CARIBOU HUNTER

CARIBOU

A SONG OF A

SERGE BOUCHARD

Translated by JOAN IRVING
Foreword by J. EDWARD CHAMBERLIN

HUNTER

VANISHED INNU LIFE

GREYSTONE BOOKS

Douglas & McIntyre Publishing Group
VANCOUVER/TORONTO/BERKELEY

Greystone Books
A division of Douglas & McIntyre Ltd.
2323 Quebec Street, Suite 201
Vancouver, British Columbia
Canada v5T 4S7
www.greystonebooks.com

Library and Archives Canada Cataloguing in Publication
Mestokosho, Mathieu
Caribou hunter : a song of a vanished Innu life / [as told to and edited by]
Serge Bouchard ; translated by Joan Irving.
Translation of: Récits de Mathieu Mestokosho, chasseur innu.
ISBN-13: 978-1-55365-157-4 • ISBN-10: 1-55365-157-X

1. Mestokosho, Mathieu. 2. Montagnais Indians—Hunting—Québec (Province)
3. Caribou hunting—Québec (Province) I. Bouchard, Serge, 1947–
II. Irving, Joan III. Title.
E99.M87M4713 2006   306.3   C2005-907520-1

Library of Congress information is available upon request

Copy editing by Iva Cheung
Cover design by Peter Cocking
Text design by Ingrid Paulson
Cover image © Christian Lamontagne/First Light
Printed and bound in Canada by Friesens
Printed on acid-free paper that is forest-friendly (100% post-consumer
recycled paper) and has been processed chlorine free
Distributed in the U.S. by Publishers Group West

Financial support for this translation provided by the Canada Council for the Arts
and the Department of Canadian Heritage through the Book Publishing Industry
Development Program (BPIDP). We also gratefully acknowledge the financial
support of the British Columbia Arts Council for our publishing activities.

For Georges Mestokosho, my true brother

CONTENTS

FOREWORD

"What I remember is a voice," begins Serge Bouchard's account of his friendship with Mathieu Mestokosho, and Mestokosho's voice is as clear on these pages as it must have been over thirty years ago when Bouchard recorded him speaking in his native Algonquian and then translated his story into French. Now it is published for the first time in English, in a fine translation by Joan Irving.

Mestokosho was an Innu hunter from northeast Quebec, the subarctic boreal forest where black spruce and white snow and gray rock shape the great Labrador watershed. It is a place routinely dismissed as a bleak hinterland, but it is transformed here into the bountiful homeland of Mestokosho's people.

Mestokosho spoke of a way of life that was passing away. He paid special tribute to the elders, Innu technicians of sacred as well as secular well-being, dreaming the hunt and doing the things necessary to make it happen, praising God and keeping their powder dry. "To be successful using their methods," says Mestokosho, "you had to believe in them."

And he does. Soon, so do we. Believing in them means moving with the seasons, following the herds, and harvesting the fur-bearing animals, settling down in the still center of their turning world. The contradiction is right there: Mestokosho and his family are constantly on the move and always in the same place—just like the rivers they travel along, winter and summer. Subsistence represents a rich and relatively abundant life for them, much more than merely getting by; it includes duties and devotions that signify a form of sovereignty, and (not incidentally) a protection against spiritual as well as material pollution.

In telling his tale, Mestokosho does not characterize what he does as extraordinary. To do so would be to accept someone else's standard. Instead, he shows us the everyday dignity of an ordinary life on the land. "To each his own work," he says, with exemplary respect. "Out on the land the whites worry all the time and wear themselves out for nothing. They're not at home. It's the opposite for the Indians."

His homemakers are women as well as men, of course. Without the work of the women, Mestokosho emphasizes, there *is* no life on the land, and he celebrates their work (which includes a good deal of the hunting) in affectionate detail. The families accompany the men on trips as long as several months, and everything they need is out there—except tea and tobacco, for which Mestokosho has an unapologetic and carefully rationed enthusiasm.

Again and again, he returns to the beauty and the bounty of the life of a caribou hunter. "My sons are hunters of game birds," he explains. "They have a pact with the Canada goose. Every Indian has his animal. For some, it's the bear; for others, the duck. Mine was always the caribou." So the caribou is the presiding spirit of his story; caribou meat gives strength and courage, and it also gives ease and contentment. In answer to a question about when and where to hunt, he says casually that "the caribou would decide." And then he goes ahead and does all the things he has to do to be ready for the caribou's decision.

Mestokosho's story is a praise song. The life it describes may have vanished, but it lives on in memory and imagination, where real things happen. And where knowledge is kept. We hear a lot these days about the new knowledge-based society. There is nothing new about it at all. It is as old as humankind; and listening to Mestokosho, we are reminded of the range and richness of his people's knowledge and of how that knowledge requires and rewards respect. In his account, hunters become like the scholars who once gathered in the ancient library of Alexandria and developed reading practices that were constantly tested against the texts available to them, shaping a tradition of strategies that were suitable to their particular territory and that also had universal significance.

Coleridge once said that the wheels of the mind catch fire by whirling. For Mestokosho, "you have to hunt constantly to have good luck." Which means unceasing craft and care—making canoes and toboggans, making camp and breaking trail, stalking game and setting traps, never wasting anything and always watching for trouble, planning ahead and learning from the past. It is a covenant in wonder with the world. It is what this remarkable book offers us.

J. EDWARD CHAMBERLIN
Professor of English and Comparative Literature
University of Toronto

PROLOGUE:
AN **ORDINARY** LITTLE **INCANTATION**

———

What I remember is a voice. Mathieu was telling the song of his life, off on his own, in a dark corner of the main room of the house, close to the stove, in his rocking chair. He spoke, recited, recounted—the sound so far in the background that no one paid any attention to it, though they all heard it and knew what it was about, knew the muted and deep music of a voice on a journey.

Mathieu was already very old in 1970, over eighty, it was said, although no one was sure of his age. This was because the missionary had baptized him several years after his birth.

His age was therefore noted in the thereabouts of another world—one where keeping count was not the primary concern of men. He was born in about 1885, in the interior near Piastie-Baie, and that was all Mathieu said about it.

Great old age, like youth, distances us from time; these are protected places where time suspends its flight; these are blessed times that flow with poetry and dreaming. Mathieu talked, talked, talked, in short measures of murmuring, in the regular drone of an incantation, in the style of an interminable prayer, breathing to the rhythm of a very long poem.

His sons had returned from hunting Canada geese and black ducks far away in the Mingan Archipelago. They had returned to Mingan—Ekuanishit—the Indian reserve, old fur-trading post, new permanent village of the Innu, on the coast. They were handsome, Georges and Moïse, driven by a strange spark of freedom, wrapped in the smells of smoke, ocean, spruce, and fog. They were simply handsome, their bodies, faces, like their sister Desneiges, who had married a Moenen, another family of great hunters, handsome and beautiful, like most of the Mestokoshos: Abraham, the eldest, and Pierre, the youngest, handsome like their mother, Marie-Madeleine, Mathieu's wife, who was much younger than him.

Abraham, Matthew, Mary Magdalene, Moses—it's amazing, the extent to which the Oblate Fathers had evangelized, literally, the Innu world.

Mathieu went to Mass every Sunday. During the week, you'd sometimes see him leave the house, circle it, touching this, picking up that, all the objects and useless gestures that evoked the long ceremony of his life. Pick up a piece of firewood, collect some branches, move something from one place to another, for no reason, for no reason. He shuffled more than he walked: like a bowling pin about to topple, he seemed to sway continually because his legs were so bowed with time, the portages, the heavy loads, and the walking.

"My sons are hunters of game birds; they have a pact with the Canada goose," Mathieu told me, proudly. "Every Indian has his animal; for some, it's the bear; for others, the duck. Mine was always the caribou. The caribou and I got along fine. My sons Georges and Moïse have the Canada goose in their heads."

Me, the budding anthropologist, a young man of the same age as Georges, I listened. I had everything to learn; I was taking my first steps out in the field. I watched and admired, naïve to the bone. I was on the threshold of a mental space very different from my own: me, the city boy, the Montrealer, the French Canadian. But the mystery is vast. I was drawn like a fish in a river current. I had everything to learn, but it was as if I already knew it. This world was as familiar to me as if I had some part of this universe within me.

"Georges, why don't you listen to your father when he talks?"

"All of the old-timers have been mumbling these stories forever. My father is telling them to himself. But he knows that we hear him, like in the tent…"

"What's he saying?"

"He's recounting his life, the life of the Elders. He's telling us things, telling us the legends. It's always the same old record…"

"We should tape-record him…"

"Yes, that'd be a good idea, and my father would like that."

A tape recorder, the voice. So simple, so easy. I penetrated the continent of Vocality, to use Paul Zumthor's expression. I wanted to learn the language, the history, and the visions of the world. But instead I learned how to live. I didn't really learn Innu; rather, I learned to speak and to hear. I learned the spectacle of life, the art of representing it, of telling it, of organizing it, of creating it. I learned, I think, poetry.

We sat at the kitchen table, drinking a beer and smoking cigarettes. Moïse entered with the geese, several geese, and cracked a few jokes. He affectionately teased the game birds, welcoming them into the hunter's house and chiding them for having been caught. Georges did not take off his boots; he was smiling with satisfaction as he showed me photographs of his dog, Gaston, the little hunting dog who was the smartest dog anyone had ever seen.

"I loved him a lot, that little dog. Dogs think, you know. Gaston was real quick, in his head. But he's dead. He was killed by some other dogs. He was too proud, and that's what killed him—his pride."

Marie-Madeleine came toward us. She had something to ask me. She spoke to her son, of course, out of shyness and necessity, so that he could translate her questions. But I understood a little of what the old woman was asking.

"How many bandits are there in Montreal? How can a person sleep at night in a place where there are bandits? How many churches are there in Montreal? How many missionaries...?"

And Mathieu, in his corner, was talking about blackflies and giants, rocks that walk, bears that sleep, big rabbits and big lakes; he talked about money and grease, foxes and martens, his brother Damien, the women, and the children.

THE INNU OF GREATER LABRADOR

Mathieu Mestokosho spoke only the Innu language. He spoke pidgin French, the useful language of the fur trade. He also spoke pidgin English, from having spent so much time at the counter of the Hudson's Bay Company on the Atlantic coast, in Labrador. But his real and sole language was Innu, which he spoke with the skill of poets and storytellers, with the creative genius of all oral peoples. In 1975, while I was working with Georges on the translation of his stories, Georges mentioned that his father spoke the language of the Elders very well and that this language was as beautiful as music from the depths of time and space.

The Innu are the people known to the early French settlers as the Montagnais and who lived throughout northeast Quebec, from Lac Saint-Jean to Labrador. The land of the

Innu covers the whole of the hydrographic basins extending to the coast of the North Atlantic and to the Gulf of the St. Lawrence, northeast of the city of Quebec. The Innu speak an Algonquian language very similar to that of the Crees (Eeyou Istchee) who occupy vast areas of the James Bay watershed. At the headwaters of each of these hydrographic basins—that is, the one draining into the Atlantic and the other into James Bay—these two peoples met, traded, collaborated, and shared a common cultural universe. Out of a taste for travel, curiosity, or something else, individuals often spent time with their neighbors on the other side of the divide between the two watersheds.

It was the genius of these nomadic peoples to cultivate the qualities of mobility and flexibility in adapting to an extremely demanding natural environment. But for centuries these qualities of adaptability and creativity went entirely unrecognized by outside observers.

Labrador, in its oldest and largest sense—that is, the peninsula that juts into the Atlantic from an imaginary line between Tadoussac and Lac Saint-Jean—is a vast taiga, a subarctic landscape of immense monotony and profound beauty—too profound to have captured the attention of passersby. The first of them was Jacques Cartier; his initial observations of the coasts of Labrador, recorded while sailing in the Strait of Belle Isle and farther along the coast, near Natashquan, set the tone for future perceptions. "I am rather inclined to believe that this is the land that God gave to Cain to punish him," he wrote. As if the terrestrial paradise of

Christopher Columbus, basking under a Caribbean sun, had its hellish opposite in the North, in the fogs rolling off the cold ocean. Abel there, Cain here.

Here was a land of rocky crags, deformed and obstinate black spruces, stunted horizons; a black land, a gray, white, and frozen land for most of the year. From the coast it seems like an infinite hinterland, an inhuman desert, this massive boreal forest without start or finish. This landscape, you realize, stretches without changing from Blanc-Sablon until the frontiers of Alaska, where it connects to the unthinkable immensity of Siberia. Cartier had brushed up against one of the most extensive forests on the planet, and one of the most ancient, made up of evergreens from the long ago age of the glaciers, living fossils—dense, hard, and small—that looked down on the oaks and ash trees because, in the universe of trees, leaves are newcomers. But none of that entered anyone's mind and for centuries, indeed right up to the present, the North American subarctic remained largely excluded from the lively story of the territorial colonization of the Americas by Europeans. Cartier, in effect, saw nothing there, or nothing more than utter misery. The inhabitants he caught glimpses of, the Innu from ancient times, could be only punished humans, lives caught on the threshold of Hell, on the brink of complete desolation.

An old idea, this idea of the insignificance of the Middle North. A tenacious idea, and a prejudice that would mark all subsequent relationships and commentaries through time. One way or another, the observer, the modern-day enthusiast, sits open-mouthed at the paucity of writing about these lands over the years, the lack of interest, the cultivated ignorance and who knows what else that ensured the missionaries, explorers, traders from the illustrious Hudson's Bay Company, and even the single-minded Oblates of Mary Immaculate would neither understand nor correctly describe the cultural universe of the aboriginal peoples of the sub-arctic, from the Innu of Labrador to the Crees of James Bay, from the Anishi-nabe of the North to the Athapaskan-Dene of the Northwest. Few were the individuals who suspected the existence of cultures interesting enough to be studied, transmitted, and shared. We suspected nothing but the errantry, the disorganization, the starvation, the misery, the improvisation, the improvidence, and we identified these peoples as small tribes of savages, nomadic tribes without codes, without laws, without faith, without rules, without boundaries.

It was thus a constant, among observers from the outside, to see desert where there was forest, to link nomadism with misery. The chronicle writers speak only of starvation, cold, and want, to such an extent that Mathieu Mestokosho's accounts are in many ways eye-opening and surprising. The land of the Innu was not just the small centers dotted along the coast but indeed the immense hinterland of Labrador. The Innu fully occupied this land by knowing every tiny parcel of it, by cultivating the immense space, like farmers cultivate their land, like fishers, the ocean, like camel caravan drivers, their infinite highways. The land of the Innu was loved by the Innu, like everyone loves their native land, large and mysterious, nourishing and insidiously beautiful. And especially, they occupied this immensity by following rules, codes, proven methods, systematized models. The errantry was not so errant. The empty was full. Their society was a real society. This is what the voice and the words of Mathieu reveal to us.

In Mathieu Mestokosho's world, authority is won, admiration is deserved, influence is tied to performance. Like many men and women before him, Mathieu sets himself as an example, and his accounts and stories constitute a sort of moral and practical bible for the apprentice nomad in the taiga. To be a great hunter in a world of hunters, this is very useful. To live well, here is what the hunter should do.

They will be punished—the lazybones, the hot-tempered, the thieves, the pouters, the blunderers, the sharp-tongued, the resentful, the loners. To be Innu in this land of hunting and trapping entails endless duties. Existence cannot be improvised, and cheaters are quickly thwarted.

You need great physical strength and know-how with respect to walking, transporting goods, mobility; brute strength, certainly, but also strength calculated in its expenditure—you journey to the rhythm of the heart and the drum. The work is always for the long haul in these immense lands of ancient spruce and rocky crags. You need to know how to think, to think well, to dream, to dream well. You need to be a master of the word in the land of Vocality, where sound reverberates in the most profound of silences. To love beauty, light, and the horizons, the star-filled sky and nights full of lunar life. You need to roll with the cold, dance with the current, breathe along the portages, and dream well when you sleep. To know your canoe, the vagaries of water, ice, currents, rocks—the details.

You need to know the animal, from its bones to its spirit. The good hunter is a scrupulous animist. The animals tell humans to stay together, with family, friends, your group. You need to love people, souls, things, and life, from black-flies to bears. And Life will reward you as one of the living and won't let you die, stupidly, before your time.

Incidentally, everything is contractual, that is, done through alliances, exchange, the flux of extratemporal energy and the transspatial, through giving and re-giving. I receive messages, waves; I see you in a dream; we understand each other. My sister, my brother, the extended family of the Living find themselves in a single song. These great hunters are artists, their art is a performance, a representation that is told, spoken, dictated, and predicted—that is, anticipated. What great dreamers these people are, these proud people, humorists, moralists, and philosophers of the eternal cycle.

Mathieu was Innu, and he lived for almost a century. His stories take us back to a world that existed between 1890 and 1960, the world of the hunter-trapper, independent and nomadic, in the vast territory of Labrador. He says not one word about the last twenty years of his life, from 1960 until his death in 1980, the period he spent on the Mingan Indian reserve in a government-built house, sitting in a rocking chair by the stove, a powerless witness to the dramas that would carry off his sons, his people, and his world when he was over eighty.

Mathieu, of course, had a long gaze. His body was in the house, but his mind was back home, back there, on the land, as he said. No one could make him leave this land that had become imaginary. He thought about nothing else, talked about nothing else. But he also appreciated the cozy comforts of his later life, which he viewed as an honorable exile. He knew that he was witnessing, through the lives of his sons and daughters, the complete disappearance of the world in which he had lived. He was neither bitter nor unhappy about it. He acknowledged the passage of time the way old people do the world over. Life was good but hard; and his children, because they'd gone to school and knew something other than the nomadic life, would never, according to him, be able to follow the ancient trails.

But he was worried. The new world that he sensed from his rocking chair and his obsessions, would it fulfill the promises of the missionaries and the bureaucrats? The new life, far from the land, in this village, despite its comforts, the heated houses, the ease—would it provide the children with a better world than the one in which he had spent his life? Old, very old—nearing the end of his life—he wasn't so sure. The unemployment, the boozing, the collective despair rampant on the reserves had not escaped his notice. He was witnessing the disaster as a powerless old man. Because the qualities that had value then, no longer served any purpose in the now.

The strength of Innu society at that time and in those spaces, in the bygone days of Mathieu, came from its adaptability, its flexibility, as well as the autonomy of the group and each of its members. The observers never knew how to grasp or correctly describe the high degree of collective intelligence that enabled the collectivity to flourish in solidarity by relying on the adaptive strength of each member. This question is very modern: the strength of the individual who is in tune with the strength of the group summarizes the whole problem of today's societies, which promote individual rights without really succeeding in maintaining the meaning of community.

To think and to walk are the same thing. To follow the current of a river in a canoe and to reflect are also the same thing. To hunt and to dream: another equivalent. Admirable men and women have these qualities finely honed: exceptional physical conditioning that enables great energy expenditure at a marathon-like pace, a meditative mental state that draws you into the self while opening you to the infinite, and sharp senses, precise movements—perfection comes to those who know what they are doing.

A large number of families spent their summers together, at Musquaro, Natashquan, Mingan, and elsewhere, at Goose Bay and Sept-Îles. They were thus reunited in a specific place, every year, during the hot summer days. But they left again in August, the month when the geese take flight. The summer-time community broke up and scattered into small family groups; no more lazing around the trading post in the shadow of the little wooden chapel on the coast, or beside a big lake where the winds blow hard enough in June and July to keep the blackflies away. The Innu traded the furs they trapped during the year for flour, tea, tools, coarse- and fine-grained cloth—a variety of items that were as specific as they were limited in range. They built and repaired their small canoes. But after two months of rest, the tents came down and the canoes took to the water in the hundreds. The families set off in August amid volleys of laughter and jokes: joy, celebration, with the Catholic missionary's aspergillum furiously bobbing up and down to bless the flotilla, the hunters firing their rifles at the sky. That was the signal to return to the land.

> The country that I love, the one whose every parcel and piece I adore, is precisely the country that you scorn.

> The country that I love, the one I cherish each and every memory of and whose deep silence I hear again, is precisely the country where you never want to live.

This is what Mathieu would have said to the community of detractors. This is in fact what Mathieu says throughout his stories. We felt good, we were good. We sensed your scorn, but we held on to our dignity: the native land is sacred. It was beautiful; we were beautiful.

They left in mid-August and their journey was long. Some groups covered as many as 500 kilometers (300 miles) before arriving at the hunting grounds where they would spend the long winter. But no one was in a hurry. The longest journey lasted two or more months, and when a journey lasts two or more months, it's no longer a journey—it's the rhythm of life. They paddled against the current, without motors on their canoes; they portaged, they hunted, and everything rolled along at the slow rhythm of determination. The places are imbued with memories, stories, and images. Labrador is familiar to the Innu in its every detail.

When they arrived at the wintering grounds, these groups of three, four, or five families lived at the heart of a large territory. There, for many months, life was routine. The women tended the fires, the children, and older relatives— the fires to which the hunters and trappers always came back. The women went ice fishing, hunted small game, snared rabbits. They took impeccable care of the main tents, looked after the children, cleaned and prepared the animal skins, and dealt with all the other rigmarole of daily life. The men were constantly on the move, checking traps and snares, and keeping watch for big game, especially caribou.

The women gave birth; the people took care of each other, healing their illnesses as well as their wounds; and they died, so often that these vast stretches are dotted with as many gravesites as there are birthplaces. The Innu depended on no one but themselves, and they didn't ask for anything. In any case, no one was keeping track of the details of their lives.

Of course, they needed the summer visit to the store, the famous fur-trading post, a chapel, and a priest, and thus the game was completed; that is, the cycle, the wheel of time, the year that unfurls with the departure, the return, and the new departure.

AND THUS IT GOES . . .

Comfort is irresistible; today's things are too nice to turn your back on. The world of Mathieu is dead and gone, all of a sudden. But its meaning survives him. The older it gets—this voice from another time—the more I hear it like a prayer, an animist formula that says trees are precious, the landscape is our soul, our dignity is at stake. Mathieu knew that the voice would never again be like before, connected to hearing. But he imagined that perhaps not everything had been lost. He told his stories into the void knowing that sooner or later we would revisit this void in order to know who we are.

Far from pious images, far from caricatures, here is ordinary and traditional humanity, with all its weaknesses and strengths. And Mathieu, like many other Innu men and women, simply wanted to say to the detractors: we were human, profoundly human. With our songs and our poems, with our shouts and our laughter, and also with our tears. And there was a lot more to it than you think.

I see him once again miming an eagle on the lookout for fish; I see him once again demonstrating with his hands how the wolverine walked on ice; I hear his voice once again talking about the hunger and the hardship: his gravity, his inflections, his stops and starts.

There were several Mathieu Mestokoshos among the Innu, magisterial men and women who were talkative, knowledgeable, and quick to smile. What was saved, was saved. The men are dead and the women are gone. But something of them remains: a philosophy, songs, sounds, poetry. Now all that remains is for us to listen, hear, understand, learn, and appreciate: the proud and solemn incantatory discourse, the representation of humane humanity, like the one we are all searching so hard for, in our time.

SERGE BOUCHARD

MAY 2004

PART **ONE**

———

ONE

MEMORIES OF YOUTH, 1895

I remember my father. I was about eight years old when he died. I was eight or maybe a little older. I remember very well when I went sliding on the snow in my toboggan near Baie-Johan-Beetz. It was out on the land, not far north of Baie-Johan-Beetz. That's where my father died and it's also where my grand-father, my father's father, lived most of the time when he was hunting. My father died there, in the spring, at the end of April. I remember that after he died the Indians took his body to Baie-Johan-Beetz and then sent it by boat to Havre-Saint-Pierre. That's where my father was buried and where he now rests.

My mother's name was Élisabeth. She remarried one year after the death of my father, to a man by the name of André Menikapo, whose nickname was Maiapeu.

My mother also died during that time. Since I had no parents, I stayed with an Indian named Joseph who had come to Mingan. I started living in Mingan with Joseph and his family when I was about nine. My brother Damien lived with Jean-Baptiste Mestokosho. Our late father was named Abraham Mestokosho.

In the beginning Damien lived with Napeshis, my grandfather's brother-in-law. My grandmother was related to Napeshis: he was her brother. So that's where my brother Damien went to stay, though not for long. He changed families often. He rarely stayed more than a few months in one place. I think he got married after being with his fifth family. The last family he was with before getting married was my late brother's. You could say that Damien fixed himself up with a lot of families when he was young. Me, I chose Joseph's family, and I stayed with him until he died.

I don't remember how old my mom was when she died, but I know she was old. She was over sixty. Before she got married her name was Élisabeth Grégoire.

At that time, when I was living in Mingan, I wasn't married and went out on the land with my grandfather Joseph. We took the Romaine River to a lake named Uauiekamau. We didn't stay out on the land all year long. We'd return before the Christmas holiday, or sometimes just before New Year's. Sometimes, after Christmas, we'd set out for a longer time, to a place named Upatauakau. It's between Naskume-kan and Upuapuskau-nipi. Back then, we hunted in this area. I was already married when we started going there. Later, after my first wife died and I married the woman who is now my wife, I started hunting and living on the land for periods of a year or longer.

Yes, after my second marriage I became a real hunter. I've spent my whole life killing animals and selling furs. Our journeys were long, especially the ones that took us to North West River. You must know Atikonak Lake…It's north of here. We'd start out there and travel east. We had to go to Winuakapau Lake and, when we arrived at the falls there, cut over to another lake. If we went farther we came to the area around North West River. It starts out as a big river, almost a narrow bay. We were always headed for the ocean. I remember the last set of falls before we arrived. We hadn't yet come to the real ocean, we were still in the woods, but the water in the bay was salty, and sometimes it was high, sometimes it was low.

It takes a long time to walk that bay on foot. In some places it's very narrow, then it becomes real wide and then narrower again.

The Indians from La Romaine often went to that area because they didn't have to travel far to get there. The Indians from Natashquan also went there fairly often. For us from Mingan, if we left in August, it took five months to go to North West River via the Atikonak and Winuakapau lakes. We arrived there in December.

We left Mingan at the end of August. Before the snow came we lived on the land and hunted for caribou, otter, and beaver so that we didn't have to use up our provisions but also because we wanted to trap for furs. We arrived at Lake Brûlé before freeze-up. We left our canoes there and returned for them when the ice broke up.

We sometimes arrived too early in the spring or before the weather had started to warm up. Then we had to wait to get our canoes. While waiting, we went hunting at Little Lake Brûlé. But as soon as the ice broke, we took our canoes and headed for Mingan. The snow would be gone, except at the portages.

In those days, living on the land was really good. Today, when I think about it all, I miss the hunting and the land where I spent my life. If you were a good hunter there'd be as much meat as you wanted. There were lots of ruffed grouse in the woods, and we always knew where to find plenty of them. Even here, in the old days, in and around Mingan, there were lots of ruffed grouse. We also ate porcupines. There were plenty of them around, too. When we were canoeing we'd often spot two or three porcupines in the trees. We'd kill them. They were very good to eat.

I was one of those who used to go to North West River along the route through the Atikonak and Winuakapau lakes. There were English-speaking trappers there, living and trapping out in the bush. They always built their log cabins a one-day walk from each other. When we saw a cabin, we knew there was another one just a one-day walk away. They were built in a line like that. Sometimes, the English-speaking trappers would sell us beaver pelts. These would be furs they'd kept a long time and couldn't sell back home. They were beautiful pelts. We had money on us to buy provisions in North West River, and these trappers wanted to sell us their beaver pelts, which were useless to them. But they kept their otter pelts because they could sell them when they got back home.

The Indians couldn't decide. I wanted to try it and I used some of my money to buy beaver pelts around there. I paid two dollars for a large beaver and fifty cents for a small one. I looked after those skins and, that summer when I was back in Mingan, I was rewarded for the risk I'd taken. The other Indians who'd decided not to buy because they were afraid there'd be no market for the fur in Mingan were very disappointed. I got thirty dollars a beaver pelt in Mingan, and as much as sixty for the nicest ones. Beaver that I didn't even kill myself and that I'd paid two dollars for! I made an incredible amount of money that time. Later, I talked about it with the missionary. I wasn't sure if it was alright to buy and sell the furs at those prices. He said that I hadn't done anything wrong because, in any case, I hadn't taken anything from the English-speaking trappers. To them, these beaver pelts were just a nuisance. In North West River, beaver was worth absolutely nothing, so these trappers were just holding on to the furs.

Marten sold well there, but the English-speaking trappers wouldn't have sold us marten at the same price we paid for the beaver. We knew that the price for marten in Mingan was very high, but we weren't sure about the price for beaver. The English-speaking trappers were saying that the days of trapping were coming to an end and that very soon even marten would be worthless. But beaver was still selling well back home.

I can tell you a lot of things about these journeys and these subjects.

TWO

THE **GREAT CARIBOU** HUNTS

LONG JOURNEYS FROM MINGAN TO

NORTH WEST RIVER, 1925

We were a group of four hunters, and we had found a large number of caribou living by these lakes. First, we discussed how we would kill them. We knew that there was a small herd on a little river. To get there, we followed the tracks of the caribou. Sure enough, there they were, and I started shooting them with Tshishapeu, the Indian from La Romaine who was with me. Tshishapeu fired first but he missed. There was a plateau near the river, and on it, not far from us, my grandfather was waiting for the caribou. Damien had been sent to wait on the other side of the plateau. We all started firing at the caribou, which split into groups of two to five caribou and fled. There were already two caribou down on Damien's side. I also killed several of them.

My grandfather asked, "Where did the other ones go?" We could see by their tracks that they'd followed a little stream. They'd made a wide trail and broken a lot of small trees. My grandfather asked me to go find them. I had on a new pair of snowshoes, and I walked all around the bay where the stream entered the lake. We didn't find anything and returned to my grandfather. He said the caribou had probably fled to a lake not too far away. Without even putting on our snowshoes, we walked across a plateau to get to that lake.

When we arrived we found the caribou. They had just emerged from the woods and were about to walk onto the ice. There were a lot of them, probably around seventy caribou. They were walking out of the trees in groups of five or ten and getting ready to lie down on the lake. The other hunter and I discussed how to kill as many as possible.

The wind was in our favor; the caribou were directly upwind of us. I climbed a small hill, being very careful not to be seen. From that hill I could see a plateau with a grove of trees on it, and it was there that I decided to hide and wait.

The caribou weren't able to run that day. The snow was crusty and deep, and when the surface broke it was very sharp. That's when I told the other hunter to go find the caribou.

There were plenty of them, some lying down on the snow, others standing and keeping watch. They were all in small groups spread out across the lake. There was a group of six caribou very close to me and I managed to kill some of them. The other hunter, who was on the lake, drove the caribou toward my grandfather, toward Damien, and toward me. Several of them headed in my direction.

It was hard for the caribou to run because of the snow-drifts on the lake and the sharp snow. I shot one by aiming at its shoulder. I then killed two others who went right by me, running side by side. I think a bullet went through the ribs of the first one and hit the second one in the stomach.

I had told the other hunter to come get me when he'd finished driving the caribou, which were climbing a bank and about to escape into the woods. They made it, but I was shooting non-stop and succeeded in killing another one, the last of the group. So about thirty of them managed to get away. We didn't go after them. Instead, we headed back to the lake where some caribou had stayed behind.

My companion ran out of bullets, so I had to lend him some. I gave him seven bullets and we each set off in different directions around the lake to kill the rest of the caribou. But we couldn't get close enough to them; they were moving around and didn't stop upwind of us. Even so, we managed to kill eight two-year-olds. Some twenty more caribou were still out on the lake. The other hunter and I met up to discuss the next move. He asked me what we should do. I told him that the caribou would decide for us.

So my companion started off across the lake without snowshoes in pursuit of the caribou. He managed to get within range and kill several of them. The rest of the caribou didn't want to leave the lake. They were searching for a treeless place to flee to. They were afraid of the trees and wouldn't go back into the woods. But this frightened herd, which we couldn't get near, wasn't all that important to us. We already had enough meat on the ice of the lake. My friend told me that we had better go cut the throats of the dead caribou. I set off on my own to slit the large veins and, when that was done, we met up.

We made a fire to prepare a quick meal because we still had a lot of work to do. We weren't far from the small lake where we'd left the women and the toboggans, so my companion went back to tell them about the hunt, since they wouldn't have heard the gunshots. Then, many hunters and women arrived to help us bleed the caribou and do all the rest of the work. On the hill were numerous dead caribou crowded together. When we'd bled them all, we drank some tea, since a fire was already burning.

My grandfather's name was Old Sylvestre. He told me to go find the wounded caribou before it started snowing and their tracks were covered. I climbed the hill and set off into the woods to find the wounded caribou. I found one already dead whose throat had been slit. I found three others like that. It was the same for my friend. He and I were really glad to come across those eight dead-and-prepared caribou. We went back to the lake where the women were butchering the caribou with their large knives. By dusk, we were all back at the camp. We'd left the caribou right where they were, taking only the fetuses that we'd found in the bellies of the females, because we weren't allowed to leave them on the snow like the real caribou. It was Easter time, and we could walk without snowshoes, right on the snow.

We all had fetuses on our backs. I was carrying seven. We crossed a stream, climbed a hill, then came back down and out on a lake. By the time we arrived at the lake it was dark. Our camp was at the end of this lake.

We killed seventy-seven caribou that day. We had killed about thirty a few days before, and our racks were full of meat. We had more than one hundred caribou to eat.

When we got back to the camp we cut off the feet of the caribou so we could hang them to dry. The next day was Sunday; all we did was eat the baby caribou. We didn't work, we didn't move. It was a beautiful day and, when night fell and it cooled down, the snow started to harden.

On the trail we'd taken to get back to our camp, I heard a noise. About twenty caribou had run onto our lake. We immediately picked up our rifles, but my grandfather stopped us, saying that we had enough caribou and that, in any case, we could shoot some the next day if we left our dogs loose during the night. Out on the lake the dogs were circling the caribou, making it impossible for them to escape into the trees. We therefore decided to let those caribou be and to get ready to go to sleep.

The next morning we broke camp and tied everything onto our toboggans. My grandfather sent me and another

hunter to kill some caribou. We set off, leaving the other hunters and the women to pull the toboggans to the lake of the
seventy-seven caribou. My grandfather had warned us not to
follow the tracks of the caribou by that lake. But we did go by
the lake to get to one that was behind it. When we didn't find
anything there, we started back to the lake of the seventy-
seven caribou. It had warmed up very quickly and begun to
rain, so we had to take cover. We arrived back at the lake
where we'd left our caribou just as the others got there with
the toboggans.

The work on the dead caribou took us a long time, but we
ended up with a large amount of good meat. That night, we
were all very tired when we went to bed. We had also had to
search the area for any dead caribou that we might have missed.
Four fires had burned all day long to smoke and dry the butchered meat. The women were in charge of that. We also had to
prepare the bones so that we could make grease from the marrow. We worked on that all day long. The snow was wet because
it was a hot day, and it was difficult to walk on.

We prepared packs of dried and smoked meat that were as
big as a toboggan. It took more than a week's work to prepare
all of those caribou. My grandfather asked the hunters to
crush the bones and make the grease. So that's what we did;
Damien crushed the bones, and I used my knife to pick out
the marrow. I also crushed bones. Damien broke them on a
rock. Old Sylvestre, my grandfather, got the bones ready for
us. He was with Tsehapeu and Thaddée. That way, all working

together, we prepared a large amount of grease. Then we ate some and went to sleep.

The next morning we ate some more grease. It was a cold day, a nice day. My grandfather decided that there was nothing more to do around there and that we needed to change locations so we could hunt otter. During the caribou hunt he'd killed an otter as well as a lynx.

My grandfather was very canny. He loved hunting and living on the land. He never let anything stop him. The week that we spent working on the caribou, he went hunting all alone in and around that area. On the lake behind us, the one where we'd lost the trail of the caribou, he found them but never told us.

So we changed camp. My grandfather and I set off first, carrying only the caribou heads. We wanted to put them on our racks a little farther away. The women used the brains to soften the skins. The rest of the head was roasted; it was very good. So we were carrying several heads. To get to the racks we had to climb a hill and go through a forest.

We stopped to make a fire and drink some tea, and the others arrived shortly after. We were four hunters. After that stop we split up. Damien and Tshishapeu were supposed to leave together. Before setting out, we all had one last meal together.

I left with my grandfather. We were planning to follow the river. As we went down the bank, we looked back and noticed that the others were crushing the heads and still eating. Later, traveling on the river, we saw the break-up of the ice and the still white surface of a little lake. It was a warm day. I looked around and noticed fresh bear tracks in the sand on the riverbank. I went over to examine them up close. It was really hot and the snow was melting.

I told my grandfather that the track was very fresh, that the bear had passed not long before. I knew exactly where it had come from; its den was a little farther along. My late brother had shown it to me once before.

To make it easier to follow this track, we left all of our packs there. My grandfather wrote a message on a wooden shovel for those behind us, asking them to take our toboggans to the little lake. Later, we learned that they never saw this message. We were already far away by the time they came across the shovel. As a precaution we had taken a little meat with us. It was very hot and soon we'd be breaking through the snow.

We walked down by some twists in the river to have some tea, since my grandfather had warned me not to chase the bear right away. I had to wait until the snow got even softer. "If you chase him now, you'll just be wasting energy because you'll both get stuck in the snow, the bear and you. Let the bear wear himself out trying to run away. He won't get far and we'll take him then."

So after our tea we crossed the river. On the other side I found some small trees around which the snow wasn't very deep. The bear tracks led to this place. I was so busy following the tracks I didn't see that the bear was well hidden and waiting there. It ran off just as I got near.

I started to follow it, walking very fast, and leaving my grandfather far behind. On a plateau I spotted the bear foundering in the snow. With each step it was getting stuck. All you could see was its head. By the time I caught up to it, it was unable to go any farther. All it could do was struggle there in the soft snow.

I waited until the bear was completely worn out and, when my grandfather gave the signal, killed the bear by shooting it in the head. Then I attached a rope to it, to pull it out of its hole. There were just the two of us to pull the bear out of that hole in the snow and drag it down to the river along a shortcut. There were some falls, and above them was the lake where we'd left the meat.

My grandfather pushed the bear with a shovel, while I pulled it from the front using a rope. We crossed a plateau close to the river. While we were stopped to catch our breath, we noticed the other hunters coming to meet us. They must have known that we needed help because they didn't have their toboggans with them, only their dogs. That bear was big. They hitched two big dogs to it and the dogs pulled along with the rest of us. It was easier that way.

We walked upriver until we arrived at our little stream. At the point where the stream joined the river, the ice was melting and there were two ducks swimming in open water. We didn't have a shotgun with us, so my grandfather told me to shoot them with the rifle. I killed both ducks. Spring had definitely arrived.

Next, we climbed back up to the lake to find our racks and leave the caribou heads on them. We then set up our tents and went looking for some good spruce boughs. We also gathered some wood to make a fire. We had our teakettles with us.

After the meal we went to get the toboggans that we'd left behind. Three of us went to get the toboggans, which weren't too far away. My grandfather stayed behind to butcher the bear. While he was cutting up the bear, my grandfather shook the sand out of its fur. That bear was big.

By the time the three of us got back, the meat had already been cut up, and we started hanging it on poles so it could dry. As we were doing this, we talked about the dead bear. We said that it would remain on the rack for a long time.

By nightfall we had finished drying the meat and putting it on the rack. I noticed that the weather was gloomy. My grandfather said, "Tomorrow, you will scrape the bearskin to remove the remaining flesh." So the next day, the three of us worked on the bearskin. My grandfather boiled the fat so we could eat it. The grease he was preparing was for us to take with us. He also dried some meat for us to take. I found other poles to hang the meat from.

That evening, the weather was gloomier than ever. The sky had completely clouded over. My grandfather said that when a bear died the weather always turned bad.

It was night and we were sleeping in the tent. In the middle of the night someone shouted that it was snowing really hard. We had been buried by the snow, which was as high as the roof of the tent. We had to dig ourselves out. We said to each other that only the bear could have done something like this. We got dressed and then dug out the entrance so we could remove the snow from the tent.

The snow stopped falling and the weather turned nice. After we'd taken down the tent, we dried the canvas. It was a beautiful day. My grandfather tied the packs of bear grease on the toboggans by placing them one alongside another. To wrap the grease, he'd used canvas from old canoes. We were supposed to return to the camp the next day; my grandfather insisted that we not forget to take the grease back to the women. In addition to the packs, we had some big pots full of grease; there would be enough for all of us.

I left with my grandfather. With the heavy snow and that large load, the going was tough. We weren't moving very fast and often had to stop. We got to the place on the river where, the day before, there'd been only a little snow. My grandfather decided that we couldn't go any farther because the snow was so deep, and we therefore put up our tent.

In November, I had set four marten traps near there. That evening I went looking for my traps. In the first one, I found a marten. There had been another in the second trap, but all I found was its tail: a fox had eaten the marten. In the third, I found a beautiful marten. The last one had also killed a marten, but a fox had eaten it, too. Without that fox I'd have done well with my traps: there had been a marten in each one.

I returned to the camp. That night the snow settled and hardened.

The next day, we left for Uipuskatauakau, a lake in that vicinity. There are practically no trees around there. Earlier in the year we'd caught a large number of small whitefish in the lake; we had smoked and wrapped them and left them on racks. But when we arrived, there was nothing, not even the racks. Nearby we saw the tracks of a marten. So someone had been there! I grabbed a marten trap and we set off. A little farther down was another lake, a small one. There was open water where the river flowed into the lake. We camped at the end of this lake.

We were there to hunt for otters. When we got settled we took our snowshoes and our rifles and walked along the shore of the lake. We were headed to some rapids and, on the way, saw an otter but didn't kill it. We walked all the way to the rapids and, on the way back, killed the otter with the rifle. That night, we ate and slept in the tent. The next day, the snow was hard and easy to walk on. We left very early. The snow had just the right amount of glide. We were headed back to join the women. We had come to the end of our hunting trip without the women.

When we got there the women were just finishing their work on the caribou. My grandfather had brought back an otter and I, two martens. The other hunters arrived after dark; they'd brought back a marten.

The next day we all worked together on the caribou. That evening, we agreed to move the meat to another location, to our next camp. We wanted to have less to transport when it came time for the real departure, planned for two days later.

The next day we were supposed to take only the meat, but it snowed all night, a little like that night with the bear. So much snow fell that the trees seemed to have shrunk. That day, because of the storm, it was impossible to go anywhere.

We therefore left with the meat on the second day, transporting it a long distance, close to a rack. The next day we returned to the first camp and, this time, managed to move with our families.

I was with my first wife then—the mother of Marie, who hadn't yet been born. I had a big load and two big dogs to help me pull it. My grandfather was with my old godmother; despite her age, she still pulled the toboggan. Damien had a dog with him and Tshishapeu was very strong. He went pretty fast, despite the huge load he was pulling. The others all had children with them. I was the only one with no children.

The others left before me. When I arrived they had been there for quite a while and had set up their camp. I'd had a hard trip because the toboggans were constantly getting stuck in the snow. They were too heavy. I therefore arrived at the destination much later than the others. But the meat that I was transporting, I never left it in the woods. The rest of them—to lighten their loads—had left meat along the trail, in the woods. While I was walking along that trail I saw their tracks veer off and head toward the woods. One time, I stopped pulling and followed the tracks. I discovered their packs of meat tied up in the trees, but I couldn't resign myself to leave meat there. Sooner or later, we wouldn't have enough meat; above all, we had to make sure that we didn't waste any of our surplus meat. The others, when they did that, certainly weren't thinking about having nothing to eat. It was dark when I arrived at the camp.

The next morning, we returned to our old camp to get the meat and packs we'd left behind. When we got there, after a long and difficult journey, we carried the surplus packs to our new camp. We stopped at this camp for a quick meal, returning home the same night. It was hard going. The next day we changed location again; we moved the tents, meat, and packs to the place where, the day before, we'd taken our surplus packs.

When we arrived at our destination, we set up the tents. I then started making a toboggan with runners. Damien and his father were doing the same thing. We finished in a couple of hours. That evening I left to get my canoe from the place where I'd left it the previous fall. I took my toboggan in order to carry the canoe, which was near a river, the Natuakami. Damien also came to get his canoe, which was in the same place as mine, but on the other side of the river. We returned to the camp together.

The next day we left with all of our canoes and all of our packs, since the snow was hard enough to support us.

It was around the end of April. I arranged my canoe so that the canvas wouldn't rip because of all the things stored under it. I had a big dog that was very useful for pulling toboggans. My wife also had a dog; hers was a little smaller. We had one other dog, a really small one. It never pulled anything. It was a small bitch that was good at hunting porcupines and grouse.

It was a long journey but it wasn't all that hard. We arrived in the evening at the place where we wanted to camp: the lake where a fox had eaten my two martens and where an animal had eaten our whole cache of whitefish.

As soon as we'd set up camp, I walked with the other hunters over to an island in the lake. We wanted to build a new rack, bigger than the last one, for our surplus powdered meat. We left several twenty-pound pots there. We also left caribou grease and many other things. We didn't need them because it was May and we were about to go to Lake Brûlé and, from there, back down to Mingan.

The next day we left once again. Without the extra provisions that we'd left on the island, we made better progress, and we were able to travel a great distance that day.

We walked for two days to get to Long Lake. I was strong, and nobody got tired out. We were all very fit. There was just enough snow still on the ground for us to use our toboggans. We traveled like that until we reached Lake Brûlé. It's a very long lake. When we arrived at the falls on the lake, we couldn't walk to solid ground. There were water holes everywhere. To get over them we needed to use our canoes.

At that place, there's a portage leading to the Romaine River.

When we saw that the ice had melted, we were all very glad. It meant we no longer needed our toboggans, no longer needed to walk. We could travel downriver in our canoes. But we didn't leave right away; instead, we set up camp and spent the night there. The next day we left and, after an easy portage (there was no more snow), we set out down the river in canoes with our packs. We didn't even stop to hunt because, as far as we were concerned, we already had enough furs for the year.

The river was very twisty. It was well known as a place for setting out fishing nets.

We were in three canoes; mine was in the middle. Suddenly, the others saw a tent on the shore of the river. In that one tent were two families. They were all inside the tent and didn't know that we were passing by. The current carried us a little beyond the tent, and we had to turn around to paddle back to it. It was my godfather Paul Nolin and my godmother Hélène Napish. They had arrived at the river just that morning. The winter had been harder on them than on us, and they were surprised to see us fit and healthy. I was as fat then as my son Moïse is today.

They were hungry and hadn't killed any caribou for some time. We had a large amount of meat and grease. They were very glad to be able to eat their fill.

We decided to stay with them—to wait for them. My godfather had traps in that area that he wanted to check. I left with my brother Joseph to go to a place a short distance downriver. We got caught in ice that had built up in a sort of bay, and to get out of there we had to portage. We then set two otter traps along the banks of the river; it was starting to get dark, so we turned around and started back.

As we paddled up the river, I spotted a lynx and managed to kill it by shooting it in the head. We put it in the canoe and set out again. When we got back to the place where the ice had blocked our passage, I saw another lynx. It was walking on the ice, trying to cross the river. The ice was making a lot of noise as the chunks smashed together, and the lynx was having a hard time getting across. It didn't see us because it was too pre-occupied. We didn't want to kill it on the ice. We were afraid we'd lose it or not be able to reach it after it died. We waited for it to come to shore, which it did. But instead of running off right away, it stopped and, still without noticing us, sat right down to think about the ice it had just crossed.

That's where it died. It was so captivated by the moving ice that we were able to get really close and kill it. By then, we were almost back at our camp. We stayed a whole week on that river, which runs from Lake Brûlé down to La Romaine.

This was in May, and we arrived at the Saint-Jean River in June. I'm going to describe the route we had to take to go from Lake Brûlé to the Saint-Jean River.

The first portage was a rather long one—it's six to seven miles long, from Uashekamu Pakatan to Uashekamu-nipi. Then there's another portage, named Matamek Pakatan, that goes to Matamekous-nipi. After that is a portage to a lake named Kashakauekakamat. Then, there are a lot of short portages before you get to Makatesh-nipi. It's a big lake. You have to cross it and join up with a river by the name of Naskauekan, which is a branch of the Romaine River. At that point, you change direction, but you're still following the Little Romaine River. That's how you get to the Romaine River, which flows into Lake Brûlé. Between the Little Romaine River and Lake Brûlé is a long journey. That's where we were, that year, in the month of May. We were on our way back to Mingan. Almost every year we were able to cross Kashakauekakamat Lake on the ice. But that time, the ice had already broken up.

We arrived in Mingan on about June 10. We had been gone a long time and had hunted all the way to North West River. We'd left Mingan in August of the previous year. We reached North West River in March, and, as I've explained, by May we were at Lake Brûlé, on our way to the Saint-Jean River. My story ends there. That's enough for today. When we got to Mingan, we didn't drink beer. There was no beer in those days. The Indians didn't drink it. This all happened a long time ago, more than forty years ago.

THREE

A WINTER IN THE **WINUAKAPAU** REGION

DESCRIPTION OF THE PORTAGES BETWEEN

LAKE BRÛLÉ AND THE SAINT-JEAN RIVER, 1930

I'll start another story. It was summer when we left Mingan
with all of our families. Much later, we arrived at Long Lake.
That's where we left our canoes because the lakes were frozen. We were a big group when we left Mingan. There was
Old Sylvestre, Damien, Bastien Basile, and Pitan Piétasho,
the husband of Thérèse Piétasho and father of Philippe Piétasho. Tshishapeu, from La Romaine, was also with us. He
had come to Mingan the previous spring. I was in the group,

but Jérôme wasn't. He was somewhere else. In all, there were seven families.

We crossed Winuakapau Lake on foot, pulling our toboggans. To stop overnight, we set up our tents on the other side of the lake. It was fall—the snow was just starting—of the year Étienne Louis' wife was born.

The next day we carried our packs to the top of a mountain near the lake. From there, we headed to an area where we thought we'd find lots of porcupines. The forest there had completely burned down and all the trees were small. It was a good spot for porcupines. I set off by myself and killed four of them by following a stream close to our camp. With what the others caught, we had twenty-six or twenty-eight porcupines. The others didn't bring back their porcupines. They had gone off to make a trail and, while doing that, had killed some porcupines, which they left behind. I was the first to arrive back at camp. The women made fires to burn the quills off the porcupines, and then to cook them. We ate our fill that night. When the others got back, they also ate well. Before that, we'd been starting to run short of food.

The next morning we left for a lake where there were some beavers that my grandfather wanted to kill. We camped there, and the men went off hunting, some of them for caribou, the rest for porcupines. We knew of a place not too far away where caribou could normally be found. There were no trees in that area—nothing but mountains and snowy hills. It took us a day to get there. The next day, we followed some caribou tracks that led us to a place named Kauastshemushuat, where there was a river. The next day, we got ready to follow the caribou tracks a long way. We had our tents, our little stoves, and the toboggans. The first night, even before we finished setting up our tents, we killed four caribou. We were close to a small lake, and the herd of about thirty caribou was headed toward a nearby mountain. The next day, we were still following their trail. We caught up with them in a forest and killed several. After bleeding them, we returned to our tents, which weren't far away.

The next day we returned for the women and children. Our grandfathers had already killed some beavers, so we all went together to the place where the men had killed more than thirty caribou. We wanted to spend Christmas there. It didn't take us long to move all of the meat to the camp, but we worked hard on that caribou meat right up until Christmas. Although we had a lot of meat, you have to remember that we were a large group.

Later, we went to visit an English-speaking trapper living in the area. We needed flour and some other things. Some of our children refused to eat meat. The trapper didn't have much, but he gave us a little flour. While we were away, the hunters who had stayed back at the camp killed six caribou.

Later, we moved to another area. Tshishapeu and his whole family left us to join his grandfather, who was hunting in the vicinity of Mistashipit.

We also went off in another direction. Near a lake that emptied in two opposite directions, we followed caribou trails and killed seven caribou. We had to build a rack in the woods to store the meat we couldn't carry. And we had to dry the meat before placing it on the rack. We knew that my godfather Puniss and the other Puniss, the father of Joachim Pawstuk, were planning to come this way. My late brother Pierre was with them, as well as Shan-Mass. They were all very hungry, but they never spotted our tracks on the lake and never found our rack. They had an old man with them who was very sick—unable to walk and on the verge of dying. Actually, they were all very hungry, but some of them were suffering more than others.

As for us, we were still traveling. To descend a steep hill with our toboggans and our packs, we left the meat behind for a few days, hanging in the branches of some trees. The other group of families had found our trail and was desperately following us. That's how they found our meat. They must have been happy and pleased to eat their fill.

At the very bottom of the hill was a river where we spent the night. Before leaving, we hung a pot of powdered meat and a bag of dried meat on a pole. We were following the river. Because of the falls and rapids, we had to portage. The journey was long and very hard because we had to walk in the woods and the snow was soft.

We arrived in an area I wasn't very familiar with, the place named "Crow's Nest," where the English-speaking trappers have their log cabins. We set up our tent near the house of a man named Willy Peggy. Pitan and I had a tent that was large enough for our two families. Damien was with his father, and Bastien Basile was with a guy nicknamed Mistikushis. That evening, we went over to Willy Peggy's to buy flour and other items. The next day, there were other Indian tents on the other side of the lake. These Indians were from North West River and Sept-Îles: Joseph André, Joseph Jean-Baptiste, Abraham, Jérôme Jean-Baptiste, and the rest. There were a lot of them and they gave us bannock and flour. The next day we finished trading with Willy Peggy, though we intended to go back later.

The others wanted to finish their buying, while Pitan's family and mine stayed home to prepare and dry our marten skins.

We left the next morning. We had brought snowshoes, but there was so little snow that we didn't use them. We walked quickly across Crow's Nest Lake, which is very long. But we hardly even noticed, since we were fit and still young. We followed our trail on the ice and, when we got to the other side of the lake, lit a fire at the same place as those who had passed there before us. After eating, we hung our tea-kettles on the branches of a tree. We still needed to cross a big bay, and we had a long way to go. Yes, the lake was very long, even if we were walking fast, without snowshoes and pulling furs that weighed almost nothing on the toboggans. We arrived that evening, just as the other Indians had finished trading their furs.

After eating we started selling our furs, continuing on into the night. The English-speaking trader had used twelve dogs and a twenty-foot toboggan to transport all of his packs. The dogs were big and strong. He had brought six barrels and some large crates filled with provisions. We met him in the middle of the big bay. He wanted to take us back home but we refused, telling him our tents weren't far away.

He replied, "Okay! That's fine," and waved goodbye before leaving. He said he'd be back the next day to give us our provisions. And true to his word, he came back.

That day, in the evening, we had a visit from Bastien, my late brother, along with Spatienis, my nephew. They arrived from the place where we'd left the dried meat for them. They had followed our trail, knowing that we had provisions. They had left Puniss behind, the man who couldn't walk anymore. His face was frostbitten, and it was impossible for him to keep going. Bastien had come looking for us to help him. During the night, we decided to leave to take them some food as soon as possible. Bastien was in a hurry because his son was back there. In my toboggan I carried flour, a half-pot of grease, and tea. We didn't take any lard, out of fear Puniss would get even sicker. We also took some caribou meat and canned meat that we'd bought at Willy Peggy's.

We started walking in the middle of the night, under a full moon. There was a lot of light. We followed the trail made by my brother and Spatienis, stopping only once to eat a little and drink some tea. We arrived at their camp at dawn. As we approached I called out to my godfather, "Are you alive?" He replied, "I'm right here and everything is fine. Come into my home." That was Bastien's tent. In the other tent there were also two families, Germain's and Puniss's. We immediately gave them bannock, flour, caribou meat, sugar, tea, and grease. But we didn't give them any lard. Out on the land, eating pork makes you weak, especially if you are sick. My godfather's name was Puniss, like the one who was sick and starving. Then my godfather got up and said, "We would be dead if you had not left behind some meat or if we had lost your trail." I told him about the rack. He replied that they hadn't seen it and that, around that time, they'd lost our trail because of a snowfall, which had covered up everything, probably including the rack.

Puniss, the one who was sick, left first, and we caught up with him later. We were returning to our camps. When I saw Puniss I shook his hand as a way of saying hello because it had been a long time since we'd seen each other. I felt sorry for him. He was wrapped up in a canvas tarp to keep warm and he seemed to be near his end. I told him that not far from here there must be a big fire going. And there was a fire, which we all sat around. We fed it more wood and cut some branches so we could sit comfortably. We made sure they had a good place by the fire. My godfather said to us, "How spirited and hard-working you are. Before we saw you, we were tired, discouraged, and weak with hunger. Just seeing you made us feel stronger." He also said that seeing one of their companions so very thin and frostbitten made them feel even worse.

That evening everyone had as much bannock, grease, tea, and sugar as they could eat. We were eating when some other Indians arrived, three men along with their dogs. It was as if reinforcements had arrived to help us take the others back—it was Damien and two Indians from Sept-Îles—so we even had enough men to transport all of the packs. The women walked on their own. When we got back to our camp, we set up their tents. My brother packed the snow to harden it so their tents would sit well.

They slowly regained their strength. When I left the next time, it was to accompany my brother, who was going to Willy Peggy's to buy provisions. But the return trip was hard because there had been a heavy snowfall and the dogs couldn't pull the crates of provisions. The dogs were riding on the toboggans and we weren't making much progress. But Kawinnut Thishennu and Michel Nolin, my brother-in-law, helped us pull our load. They were camped near there.

When all that was finished we got to work and made preparations to move to another area. We followed our ancient routes. We wanted to find another good place to set up our tents. When we found one, we started by moving the packs and the supplies to this place. It was near a small hill where there was a bear's den.

That day, Bastien Basile got out his rifle to go take a look at the den. All he took with him was his ax and a shovel. Looking at the den, he realized that a bear was sleeping inside and wondered how to get it out. So he started shoveling away the snow blocking the entrance. The bear woke up, crawled to the top of the passageway, and stuck out its head. Bastien hit it on the head with the ax so that, as we later saw, the bear's brain spilled out of its skull. Thinking that the bear was dead, Bastien walked down the hill, retraced his steps on the ice, and arrived back at our camp.

The next day we set up our tents close to the den and went to take a look at the bear. The old hunters had brought some rope and, as we walked toward the den, we heard them talking and saying that the bear probably wasn't dead. We pulled the bear out of its hole by wrapping a rope around its neck and pulling it down the slope. The bear wailed, since it wasn't yet dead. We gave the bear to Puniss, my godfather. Hearing the moans of the bear, Puniss hit it on the head a few times to kill it. But the bear didn't stop moaning and we had to keep going. My godfather wrapped the bear in some tarps, tied them well, and started to pull with the help of a dog. It was a nice day; the days were starting to get longer. The old hunters walked behind us, stopping often because of the sounds the bear was making. Finally, they stopped worrying about the wailing bear, thinking it would die soon. But instead, the bear seemed to revive and began to wail even louder.

My godfather didn't like that because the bear was wailing like a man suffering and about to die. So my godfather took out his knife, cut the ropes tied around the bear, and stabbed it in the heart. He then cut open its chest and pulled out the heart. After that, the bear stopped wailing.

The next day I went hunting up a small river we had passed the day before. At the top of the falls, I saw three otters. I killed two, immediately pulling them out of the water so they wouldn't go over the falls. I also killed the third one but it got swept away; I lost it under the ice.

As I was returning with my otters, I noticed that a bear had broken off some bushes the previous fall. I said to myself that there must be a den nearby. After looking for a long time, I finally found it. I dug out the entrance and cut two long poles so I could find out if the bear was really in there. With one pole I wasn't able to touch the other end of the den where the bear must have been sleeping. Even with two poles end-to-end, I couldn't. So I returned to the camp and told the others about it. They said to leave that bear alone, to let it sleep, because it would start wailing like the other one if we killed it.

We had to go somewhere else, and we had a lot to move. We moved the packs one day and changed camp the next. In this new place we went hunting and to explore the vicinity. I killed another otter that evening. The others had discovered the tracks of some caribou, so we had to change camp again in order to be closer to them. We camped on the shore of a large lake surrounded by trees. The next day, the other hunters and I followed the tracks of the caribou and killed eight big males. The old hunters said that the females had to be nearby. So, after bringing back the caribou meat, we left the next day to kill more caribou. My late brother noticed thirty caribou on a plateau between two mountains.

The next day everyone left to go look for those caribou, except the women; they stayed in camp to dry the meat. After walking for several hours, we located them near two hills. Two of us climbed each hill to watch the herd and give the signal to shoot. Very close to us was a steep slope where the caribou wouldn't risk going. One of us started walking toward the plateau. My late brother and Damien took position farther away, as did Germain and Pitan Piétasho.

Spatienis and my grandfather were among the men positioned with me. We had almost encircled the herd. It was Puniss who started shooting, but he missed almost every shot. The herd grew confused and, not knowing where to make their escape, headed straight for us, so Pitan and I started firing. With each shot a caribou fell. After all the caribou had been killed, the old hunters started to clean them. Not far from there were some bare hills, treeless hills, but on the plateau, right near us, was lots of dry wood that we gathered for a fire.

The old hunters told us to set up the tent. It was warm and raining softly on the wet snow. Damien, Spatienis, and I put up one big tent behind a rise, to cut the wind. There were three families and three stoves. Because there were so many of us, we arranged a second door. Fir and spruce boughs covered the floor of the tent. Then we cut some wood to keep us warm and lit the stoves. There was a small pond nearby that supplied our water. We had just finished our work when the old hunters arrived with the caribou fetuses, which they laid in the middle of the tent. We then boiled a lot of caribou meat, and everyone ate their fill.

After the meal, my grandfather picked up the rope that had been tied to one of the caribou fetuses and asked the other hunter seated by him, "What was the rope for, since we had bags to carry the fetuses?" The others, who were seated in two rows, each facing the other, replied that it wasn't them. "Well, who then?" demanded my grandfather. And Puniss replied, "It was me and there's no point talking about it any longer." But my grandfather snapped back that he must know that no one has the right to transport a caribou fetus without covering it in a bag. "We will have a cold north wind because of your error. We aren't very well sheltered from the wind here. It's a desert."

Puniss said to my grandfather, "I didn't want to stain my coat with blood." Puniss was wearing a white coat that he wanted to keep clean.

After the evening meal we cut the caribou fetuses in half so we could dry them. Then we went to bed. It was almost dawn when the north wind started blowing. Our tent was solid because we had piled a lot of snow along the bottom, and the wind had hardened the snow. My grandfather then said to Puniss, "I told you there'd be a cold north wind."

The next morning we didn't really know what to do. It was extremely cold. In addition, there were still some caribou in the area and we had to kill them. The old hunters decided that we'd go out looking for these caribou. But Shan-Mass and some of the young men decided instead to return to the camp where our women and children were waiting. We stayed behind to find the other caribou. There were still several of us. With Shan-Mass were the young men: Thaddée, Atuanis, Simon, Panape, and Pien. We were also a big group: my grandfather Sylvestre Napish; my godfather Paul Pawstuck; my late brother Zacharie Mestokosho; Damien Sylvestre; Peter Piétasho; Bastien Thomas; Paul Nolin; Bastien Basile; and me, Mathieu Mestokosho.

So, all together, there were nine of us going caribou hunting. At first, we walked in the trees to make sure that the caribou didn't see us. From time to time we stopped to rest and warm up. During one of those stops, at a place well sheltered from the wind, one of the men scanned the nearby hills. After spotting some caribou, he immediately signaled us and, with his finger, showed us where they were. There were eight caribou and we killed them all. Since they were high on a hillside, we had to take them down to the bottom, to a spot that was sheltered from the wind. The weather was nice; the wind was dying down.

After we'd cleaned all of the caribou, we headed straight back to our camp, where the women and children were waiting for us. We stopped over at our other tents only to drink some tea and to eat. Then we headed back to our families.

The next day we had to take down our tents, pack up, and move to the places where we had killed first eight caribou, then thirty, and finally the eight more, at the bottom of that hill. In all, we had a lot of meat. When we arrived back at these places, the women started drying the meat, keeping up with whatever we brought back.

The next day, with the help of the women and children, we finished our work. We had been able to move all that meat so fast because there were many of us and the work had gone quickly. We stayed for about a month at that place, then the group split up. The others went in the direction of Winuakapau. We took our families and headed toward a place where we had killed caribou in the past.

In the evening, after setting up our tents, Damien Sylvestre and I went to take a look around the area. That very same night we killed six male caribou in a herd of eight. The other two ran off; they ran so fast that we didn't even have a chance to fire at them. It was a barren land, with nothing but snow until the horizon. In addition, there were only two of us, Damien Sylvestre and me, but we now had a surplus of meat. After cleaning the caribou we returned to our camp. Before killing these caribou we had left some well-wrapped dried meat in a certain place. When we got back we told the others that we'd killed six caribou.

The next day we left with our families for the place, farther away, where those caribou were. And that's where we set up our tents. We went to get the meat that very evening because the days were starting to get longer. It was, I think, the month of April. The snow had hardened after it got dark and we were able to transport the meat in our toboggans. Damien, his father, and I each had two caribou to transport.

When the work was finished, I picked up my quarters of meat and put them on the rack we'd built. I think I set aside two caribou shoulders for drying and put the rest on the rack.

Then my grandfather said to us, "Go take a look around the area. Maybe you'll meet some other Indians who might be out of meat. We have a lot of meat to transport." He sent us in the direction of a lake named Keshikaskau. Near it was a mountain, and we knew Keshikaskau Lake was on the other side of that mountain. From the top of the mountain we saw the lake. It was big. We looked very carefully and saw a tent beside it. Then we climbed down the mountain to go take a closer look.

Two families were living there in one large tent. When we arrived at the tent, only the women were there. I knew one of them, Agnès, the daughter of an Indian from North West River whose nickname was Kawinnut Thishennu. He was my relative, my uncle. Agnès told me they were low on food. The other woman, Pinamenis, was working on a caribou skin. She was scraping off the fur using a caribou-bone knife.

Pinamenis was the wife of Tshukapeu. Agnès said to us, "The skin you see here is from the only caribou the men have been able to kill, and we have nothing more to eat. We have almost no provisions left. We're well into our last sack of flour. There are eight of us and all we have left is one pot of grease, and it isn't even full. We're almost out of tea, as well."

They got their provisions at North West River, you know, where the trader didn't want to give them much in the way of provisions.

We said that we were also short of provisions. Then we ate some meat she had cooked. She also offered us some bannock. My brother-in-law Michel Nolin was away hunting otter at the other end of the lake. We were eating the caribou he had killed that very morning at the end of the lake. It was a female that wasn't carrying a fetus.

The group had been on the move all the time, looking for caribou, but hadn't found any, except the one killed that morning. They told us that they were also fishing, using a net under the ice. A little while later Agnès noticed that her husband was on his way back and she said to me, "Your brother-in-law is coming."

As soon as he got close to the tent, he recognized me and shouted, "My brother-in-law is here!" We were glad because it had been several years since we'd seen each other. He told me about his bad luck and admitted that they had almost run out of food. I said that we were in the same situation. Then he started telling me about the otter hunt. He hadn't seen any, but that morning when he'd gone to the end of the lake to wait for them, he'd killed the caribou. It had been all alone.

His wife, Agnès, gave him something to eat. Then we stretched out to smoke some tobacco that Damien Sylvestre and I had brought. My brother-in-law also had some. A few minutes later we heard some footsteps in the snow outside. The other hunter, Joseph André from Sept-Îles, whose nickname was Tshukapeu, had returned. He had gone to the falls on the lake to see if he could find a caribou trail. Unfortunately, there had been no trail, nothing at all. Arriving at the tent, he took off his snowshoes, hung them on the side where he slept, and came inside. He was surprised to see us and said, "Well, well, visitors. It's too bad that we're short of provisions. Did you think that you might be able to eat lots of meat here? All we have left is this one caribou. It's not our fault; we just aren't lucky."

Before we went to sleep that night, they told us they planned to move their fishing nets to another place on the lake. The next morning, after we'd eaten, we went outside and I told them I was going to leave. My brother-in-law Michel Nolin pointed his finger in the direction of a lake named

Mishikamau, which was nearby. He also pointed to a mountain where there were, he said, a lot of marten. The mountain was named Uapistanami. He said, "It's to that mountain that we'd like to go when we finish here. There are often caribou there. But in our present situation, without provisions, that'll be impossible."

"You're right," I told him.

"Without provisions we could never have come to this area like the other Indians who used to come here," he said.

"You know, there's a lake near here called Uatsinakaniskamau, for the larch trees all around it. We spent Christmas at that place, which I know very well. It's where we left our canoes last fall and it's where we're staying now, with our families. Three days ago we killed six caribou there. If you don't have anything to eat, come join us there with your families. Come and get some meat—we'll give you some," I told him.

"Alright. Today, we'll set our fishing nets here. Tomorrow we'll set them in another place. And the day after we'll be at your place."

With that, Damien Sylvestre and I left. When we got back to our camp we worked on the caribou bones to make grease for the guests who would be arriving. The next day we continued breaking caribou bones and boiling them so that we could scoop out the grease. On the third day, around noon, our guests arrived with all of their packs. It was our children, playing outside, who saw them walking toward us over the ice.

We had made a big pot full of grease. When they ate, they almost emptied that pot. Those people were used to eating grease and they ate a lot of it. That evening we all ate together, finishing off the pot of grease. But we still had a good supply for ourselves because we had so much. Ours was frozen, while the grease we ate that day wasn't. It was during the evening meal that my grandfather took charge of distributing the grease, making sure not to leave anyone out. Some time before, my grandfather had prepared the grease from the thirty caribou and had given my godfather his share. So our guests ate grease but also, for a change, some powdered meat.

The next day they informed us that they'd leave the following day. Tshukapeu—Joseph André—sang and played a drum, and all of the old hunters also sang. We listened to their singing. It was beautiful.

The next day they made preparations to leave. But before that we all ate caribou grease and meat. Then my grand-father said to Tshukapeu, "Get some grease and take it with you. You'll be able to eat some more." And I told my brother-in-law Michel Nolin that I was giving him meat from two racks so his group would have meat to eat. We also gave them two nice caribou hides so they could make snowshoes. Damien Sylvestre gave a hide to Tshukapeu, and I gave one to Michel Nolin. They didn't have any snowshoes and were starving. I wonder if they would have survived if they hadn't killed that one caribou. In any case, with what we'd given them, they had enough to last until spring. We kept only a few quarters of meat for ourselves.

The next day it was our turn to leave. We left our guests behind because they had a lot of packs and meat to transport.

We set out for one of our other racks, arriving there in the evening. As we were setting up the tents we saw an otter running across the lake in our direction, so we released our two dogs. There was a terrific battle. One of the dogs took hold of the otter's neck, the other, the tail. When they pulled, each in a different direction, the otter was stretched right out. I ran over and killed it with one blow to the head. We gave the otter to my grandfather.

The next day was Easter Day and we didn't do anything. All we did was prepare our packs and put the meat from the rack in our canvas bags.

We left the next day. We had a long way to go, but the journey was easy because our toboggans glided well over the hard snow. We walked three days without stopping to get to the end of Uipuskakamau Lake, which is close to Long Lake. We had left our canoes there. And this is where we met Peter Piétasho, who had also left his canoe there.

For three weeks, while we waited for the break-up of the ice on the lakes, I hunted with Peter Piétasho at this place, named Kapapukupan. I killed four otters and Peter killed one. One day, as we were going down the river, we saw three otters. He shot at them but missed, and the otters scattered. Peter shot again, missing them once more. Then we set the traps, and I caught in my traps the three otters that Peter had missed. The otters had lead shot in their bodies, but the shot hadn't been large enough to kill them. Peter hadn't used large enough shot in his gun and I then caught all three otters in my traps. We continued on down the river without seeing or killing anything else. We went to check our traps only once, and because there were no otters or other fur-bearing animals in them, we gathered them up. We spent several days in the area.

We had food but no tea or tobacco. We did have some salt and grease. That day was probably Ascension Day. Peter had said to me, "Tomorrow, we'll hear the calls of waterfowl." In the morning I was the first one up. There was no wind. I listened outside and it was like music: a flock of migrating game birds had landed on the river very early in the morning. I woke Peter and said, "Listen, can you hear the birds? We have no more grease to eat, but we'll catch some of them." So he got up and we each took our canoes. Peter said, "You go around them, and when they fly up I'll shoot them." But they saw us and flew away before we had a chance to shoot.

I then headed for a small bay. When I got there I saw some old-squaw ducks sitting on a small piece of ice. I carefully paddled toward them. When I got within range I fired at the flock. I killed eight, but the last one was carried away by the current. I then canoed over to the other side of the river where I'd heard some geese coming. I prepared my powder gun. There were four geese. I fired, killing one of them. After retrieving it I went home. I was the first one back, and I wrapped my kill in some canvas. Peter's wife collected wood to make a fire to clean them. When she saw the ducks, she made a fire to singe and cook them.

All of the women were outside. I was inside the tent, along with Peter, who was sleeping. Suddenly, the women saw a black animal climbing a tree. I stepped out of the tent, and the women said my dog had chased it. I picked up my gun and walked toward the tree where the animal was perched. I saw a marten that was black all over looking down at me. I aimed, shooting it in the head. It fell out of the tree and I picked it up. It was so black that it looked like an otter. Peter's wife went and woke him up, saying, "Wake up, Mathieu just killed a marten that's black all over." I showed the marten to Peter. He stared at it and said, "You're always lucky."

We were at the end of Long Lake, at a place named Kauepauakaishit, where we had a rack on which we'd left meat and many other things, including the rest of our ammunition. We left the next day using our toboggans because there was still a lot of ice on the lake. It was a long journey— the lake was long. We stopped at a place named Pukuanipanin and made a fire so we could eat. The days were getting longer; it was the end of April. After eating, we set off again. At the end of the day we stopped again, this time to set up camp at a place named Natuashishau. The next day we stopped at Katsheuia-pistinakan to make a fire and to eat. It was already summer, and we were traveling by canoe. In the evening, when we arrived at Atuakamiu, we saw the others, who had come from Atikonak Lake to join up with us. In the group were my god-father Puniss, Shan-Mass, Spatienis, and my late brother. I think there were only those four, along with their families. In our group were Damien Sylvestre and his father, Peter Pié-tasho; me and my family; as well as all of the children.

The next day, after storing the things we didn't need any longer, we set off in several canoes. We were at the end of Lake

Brûlé, that is, at the head of this lake. There was still a little ice on the lake, but the wind had pushed it to the far shore. We stopped to eat on an island called Kupeshiu. Not far from it was another island where seagulls laid their eggs. We paddled over to search for eggs, but there weren't any.

After this stop, we set off again. There were eight families traveling in eight canoes. We had to make two short portages to get to a large lake named Uatikau. We crossed that lake and paddled along the shore. The lake was calm; there was no wind. It was evening and we were paddling all in a row, side by side. All of a sudden we heard a whistle and a rumbling sound. It was a tornado. It appeared a short distance away, and we could see the water churning, so we paddled really hard to get to firm ground. Climbing out of our canoes, we turned to watch the tornado, but it was already lost to sight and gone. Not far from there a small river drained into the lake. When we got to it, we crossed the lake. If the tornado had caught us in the middle of the lake, we would have capsized.

We were within sight of a short portage, which we crossed before reloading the canoes and heading toward Little Lake Brûlé. It was already evening when we arrived there and stopped for the night.

Early the next morning we loaded our packs into the canoes; we didn't have many. Then we canoed down the river from Little Lake Brûlé. There was no more ice. We paddled all day without stopping and without seeing either animals or other Indians. Finally, we came to the river we call Kukumes. There's not much water in this river, and we usually have to pole up it. But we were traveling downstream. We stopped to eat at the foot of the rapids. There's a grave at this place. A long time ago someone died there. He chose that place because everyone uses this route to return to the land or to travel down to Mingan. We stopped for about an hour to pray at the gravesite. Then we left for Kanetinat, where we had racks on which we'd left some provisions. After eating we continued our journey. That night, because we weren't in a hurry, we stopped at Kaumuakuenant to camp.

The next morning it was still dark when the old people launched and loaded their canoes. I shouted at Peter Piétasho, "Don't you hear the ruckus that the old people are making?"

He replied, "Let them go; there's no need to be in such a rush." So after eating we took down our tents, loaded our canoes, and put them in the water. We left behind our cookstoves and took only the packs. The old people were already far in the distance when we started off. By late morning we could see Kupetinatshuak in the distance. Not far from there was a portage. That's where we caught up to the old people, just as they were putting on their packs. Ours were already on. I picked up the canoe with the packs attached to it and started walking. When we arrived at the lake, I put the canoe with the packs into the water, then took the packs my wife was carrying. The others arrived at the lake in ones and twos, but the old people still hadn't arrived. We immediately started out. We could see the next portage in the distance and crossed it quickly. Not far from it was another portage, which in Innu is named Keshuekueshit. It was long. We had to rest in the middle of it, but we finally came to the lake. The slowpokes still hadn't arrived. We set off in our canoes, and a little later arrived at the portage named Katikatauakat, because you have to climb a steep hill there. We sat down to wait for the others, but after a few minutes went ahead and crossed the portage, which was a bit long. Quite a while later we arrived at the river. We had to go up this river but there wasn't enough water in it, so we had to use our poles and paddles to push the canoes along. After making our way up the river, we arrived at the portage named Makatsheu. The trail was good, and it didn't take us long to cross the portage. The others decided that when we got to the lake we'd stop to make a fire and wait for the rest of the group.

The first one to arrive lit the fire. When everyone was there, we had something to eat, then gathered up our things. We put the leftover tea on the pole on which we'd hung our teakettle. We were ready to go when the old people finally arrived. They said, "Wait for us. Don't be in such a rush." We replied, "This morning it was you who were in a rush. It was still dark when you set out." We waited until they had eaten, then left all at the same time.

The next portage was long. It came out on a narrow but very long lake. Then we came to a short portage, a small lake, and another short portage. After crossing the latter, we stopped on the shore of the lake to rest and wait for the others, who were traveling really slowly. We made a fire. The others arrived much later, and they rested and ate.

We left all together to cross the lake, heading for the falls at a place named Kashistaushekat. This portage was very hard because of the big boulders all along it. You had to walk very carefully over slippery rocks, but you could keep the canoe in the water. As you were climbing, you had to be careful not to let rocks roll down after you because they could crush those following behind. Today, I think, rocks are completely blocking this route we once used to take.

The descent was just as hard, but at the bottom was a good river that we could canoe. We left some things there that we didn't need any longer. We had racks at this place so, after eating, we put some of our packs on these racks. Then we set off for the next portage, named Little Kashistaushekat. It was similar to the preceding portage, though not quite as hard.

Some Indians took other routes to avoid these two portages. They were really hard. It took several hours to do each one. But we ended up back on the river, which we canoed down to some small rapids.

This took us to another portage named Kapapukanamistipant. But before we crossed this portage, we stopped. I was smoking my pipe when someone noticed the others coming toward us. Seeing them, we hurried to start down the portage. But the old people arrived before we'd left, and the women shouted, "Wait for us. Don't run away!"

It was my godmother and grandmother calling out. While they were unloading their packs, I was already carrying my canoe over the portage. I had almost arrived at the top when I

heard the women shout once again. This time, they were saying that one of the men had just twisted his ankle. They were
talking about my grandfather Sylvestre. He could still walk,
but couldn't carry any of the packs. All he could carry was his
canoe. I waited for him. When he caught up to me I noticed
that he'd wrapped his ankle with a red handkerchief. The old
people were tired and wanted to rest at the foot of the next
portage. It's true that it was a long journey.

We stopped on the other side of the lake, close to a short
portage and along a stretch of beach. It was a very pretty place.
You could see the whole lake. And it was a beautiful day.

After a long rest we all set off together. There were eight
canoes on the lake. We arrived at a river named Kaupauakat,
for its long sandy shoreline. The river was very low. Following
it, we came to a big lake. We paddled down the middle of the
lake and stopped at the end. Indians had been stopping at this
place for years and years: you could see several old campsites.
It was a good place to camp.

The group had to split up so we could camp there. I went
and set up my tent close to two other families, at the foot of
the portage. Not far from there was an island. My late brother
was camping there with young Bastien.

I built a cone-shaped tent. Then we ate. It got very cold
during the night, and in the morning everything was frozen.

Very early the next morning, before dawn, we heard the
old people canoeing past us on the lake. To poke fun at us,
they were making lots of noise with their paddles. Pitan and I

reassured the women, saying that we'd be able to catch up to them because they'd have to break the ice on the lake.

Late in the morning, after having eaten and prepared our packs, we also left. The sun was already high in the sky. We crossed a bay beyond which the lake widened out. We could see the old people far off in the distance, but we easily caught up to them. They were breaking the ice using poles. All we had to do was follow their path! And by then it was late and all of the ice had started to melt.

We came to a portage that we crossed without waiting for the old people. It took us to a lake where all of the ice was melted. So that was good. We crossed the lake, and on the other side was a portage trail that was not well maintained. It was full of trees and bushes. We therefore decided to take another, shorter route. The trail there was clear, except there were several hills. We had to climb those hills, but it wasn't too hard. We arrived at a small lake that we crossed. Once again, when we got to the other side, we didn't follow the old portage. We were making good progress and didn't stop once. It was a bit like a race. The three canoes of the old hunters and their families were behind us.

This portage led us to Matamek-nipi. After crossing the lake, there's a portage that's hard to forget because of the stream that crosses the path right in the middle of it. Then we arrived at a river we had to cross. On the other side, along another portage, after a series of little hills, we saw a big mountain named Kapapukupant. It was named that because a landslide had carried away half the mountain. The Matamek portage is very long. We had to walk at least seven miles—a distance equivalent to the one between the villages of Mingan and Longue-Pointe-de-Mingan. I think it was even a bit longer.

At the end of this portage we stopped to rest. We made a fire and had something to eat. We then left food and tea so that the old people would be able to eat quickly when they arrived.

As we were leaving, while we were tying on our packs, two women suddenly appeared on the trail. Although they were still far away, we could hear them shouting at us, telling us not to go so fast and to wait for them. So we did.

Later, we left all together. We had to cross a lake and make a portage to get to Matamek-shipu. We were able to canoe quite a distance on the river. Usually, the water there was low and we had to move rocks on the river bottom so that we could pass with our heavily laden canoes. But this year, it was fine; the river was high. It was the month of June.

After running a short set of rapids, we could quietly paddle the river. We canoed for a while, then came to two portages, one right after the other. The first was named Kashistaunatiskat and the second, Uashekamu.

The trees were starting to bud. The latter portage is one of the longest on this route. We didn't stop after it, but instead continued on for some distance, until we came to the Little Kaiastatautshepantit River. We rested a long time there. Once again, we were ahead of the others. We waited for them but they didn't arrive, so we left. We ended up at a place where many small trees were just starting to grow. I think that today those small trees must be very big; we wouldn't be able to walk where we once did.

Our journey was not yet over. We climbed a mountain, then managed quite easily on the downhill. But at the bottom, we still had some distance to go to get to the lake. When we did arrive on its shores, we stopped to wait for the others. Hearing them coming, we put our canoes in the water and, without waiting, set out across the lake. We wanted to get to the falls and start a fire, as we had all planned.

Sitting around this fire, we rested for a moment with the old people. We still had a long way to go, so the stop was not a long one. We had to do another portage. We were heading for a lake that we had to cross before arriving at another long portage, named Kaminuatauakat. This took us to the Uapuapatshuashu River. Still farther along, we came to a short portage on our right, and then another, longer one. It led to the river, where we encountered some rapids we were able to canoe down.

A ways down this river we had to do a portage that led to a large lake. We crossed the lake lengthwise, since the next portage was at the other end. This trail took us up a mountain. At the top we stopped for a rest and to give the old people a chance to catch up with us. We could see them far away in the distance. Without waiting for them—and knowing they were still behind us—we once again shouldered our canoes and packs and started off.

We arrived at Kashipuatetauakau Lake, where we stopped to eat. The trail dipped down to the shore of the lake, and there was a pretty place there to rest. Some other Indians had stayed there before us; it was a well-used place. We were just finishing eating when the others in our group arrived. They said they were very tired. We didn't want to stop over at this place because there were only two more portages to go before arriving at the Saint-Jean River.

It was their turn to eat. We waited for them because we knew we had to stay together to get around the falls on the Saint-Jean River. So after they had eaten we all set out together on the lake. The start of the first portage was right where the lake gets narrower. It was a very short portage, and we didn't really need to follow the trail. Then we canoed for quite a distance before arriving at the last portage, which is hard, long, and uphill. On the other side of the summit, the trail down was steep, but that's how we got to the Metapestakan River.

Once again we had to wait for the others. We wanted to canoe the river together because it's dangerous in that spot. The river flows between high banks, and there are many big eddies. You can easily smash into rocks there, and you have to canoe right down the middle of the river where there aren't as many eddies and big waves.

It was getting late. We had agreed to set up camp farther down the river; we wanted to get all the way to Washekamau Island. So we started paddling. After traveling some distance, we came to Utinaskushu. There are eddies there and it's a dangerous place to canoe. Peter Piétasho went first, trying to stay in the middle of the river. We went next. Canoes shoot right through there, and there are whirlpools on each side. But no one ran into trouble. After those rapids there's a curve in the river. We arrived at Uapmistikuetshuan but didn't stop. We were traveling very fast, almost as if we were running away from someone.

The Indians who wintered around there didn't canoe through these rapids. There's a trail to bypass them. We stopped at the start of this trail. The river is very deep at this place.

We climbed out of our canoes. The women cooked some bannock. I had no tent with me. I'd left mine behind and was planning to use it next winter. So I made a kind of shelter using canvas tarps. I didn't have my little stove, either. The others had all of these things.

Other Indians had camped there. They'd left some time ago, which we knew by examining the trees they'd cut. I'm referring to the late Jean-Louis and William Jérôme.

The next morning the old people left as usual, before dawn. But this time Peter Piétasho and I were ready at the same time as them. So we all started off down the river. The old people were up front. All of a sudden, at a place named Kapiskuamis-kat, they called out saying they'd seen a tent on the shore.

The people inside the tent were still sleeping. We shouted loudly when we went by to wake them up. They must have wondered who was shouting at them from the river! They pushed back the tarp that served as a door, and we watched as they stepped out. My grandfather went over and asked if they'd like to travel down the river with us. A little farther on there was a big curve in the river, and then it ran straight for quite a distance.

We were close to the Atshuk portage. I already had my canoe and my packs on my back when the Indians we had awakened arrived. They must have set off immediately. For them to catch up with us so quickly, they'd certainly had to hurry.

We arrived together at the Little Saint-Jean River, at the place where some [Hudson's Bay] bosses have their cabins.

We saw a beaver on the river but didn't have time to kill it. Behind us, the others shouted at us to stop. But we weren't interested in this beaver. My bullets were at the bottom of my pack and I didn't want to hunt anymore.

We then arrived at Kapemistauatshetshuant, where we ate before setting out again. Around noon we arrived at the ocean, at the village of Saint-Jean. We set up our tents, expecting to stay only as long as it would take to find a rowboat to take us to Mingan. And that evening we found one. It belonged to a white we nicknamed Uapush. He used it to transport goods from the riverboats to the village.

His rowboat was large enough to take everyone in our group as well as all of our packs. We attached our canoes to the back of the boat. The trip took two hours.

When we arrived in Mingan it was as if we were newcomers, we'd been gone for so long. We caught up on all the news, everything that had happened while we were away. And everyone settled in, put up their tents.

My family and I lived in a house, the old dispensary. I didn't need a tent. That evening, we went to the store to buy everything we needed and to get information on the price of furs.

The next morning, at about nine o'clock, we arrived at the store to sell our furs and pay our debts. At that time it was the bosses from the Hudson's Bay Company who purchased our pelts. It had been a good year: I was able to pay off all my debts. The others, too.

After that the only thing we had to do was wait for the priest to arrive. He was in Mingan only one week each year. We took communion only once a year. Yes, that's what it was like back then. By mid-June, all of the Indians had arrived back in Mingan. We were the last ones to return to the village. This is the end of my story.

TOP LEFT: Seasonal camp with clothes blowing on the line (MUSÉE RÉGIONAL DE LA CÔTE-NORD, SEPT-ÎLES, FONDS PAULINE LAURIN, NO. 1994.258).

BOTTOM LEFT: Couple and boy, with group of boys in the background (MUSÉE RÉGIONAL DE LA CÔTE-NORD, SEPT-ÎLES, FONDS PAULINE LAURIN, NO. 1994.245).

ABOVE: Twins Adéline and Napoléon Mollen, children of Sylvestre Mark, Mingan, 1953 (MUSÉE RÉGIONAL DE LA CÔTE-NORD, SEPT-ÎLES, FONDS PAULINE LAURIN, NO. 1994.58).

ABOVE: Patrick Mark and his daughter at La Romaine, August 1953 (MUSÉE
RÉGIONAL DE LA CÔTE-NORD, SEPT-ÎLES, FONDS PAULINE LAURIN, NO. 1994.256).

TOP RIGHT: The Peters family, Saint-Augustin, 1951 (MUSÉE RÉGIONAL DE LA
CÔTE-NORD, SEPT-ÎLES, FONDS PAULINE LAURIN, NO. 1994.134).

BOTTOM RIGHT: Edmond Napish and his wife preparing a seal skin, Mingan, 1964
(WILLIAM F. STILES, NATIONAL MUSEUM OF THE AMERICAN INDIAN, GEORGE GUSTAV HEYE
CENTER. © 2004 SMITHSONIAN INSTITUTION).

Around Mingan, 1951 (MUSÉE RÉGIONAL DE LA CÔTE-NORD, SEPT-ÎLES, FONDS PAULINE LAURIN, NO. 1994.136).

Ceremony blessing the canoes (MUSÉE RÉGIONAL DE LA CÔTE-NORD, SEPT-ÎLES, FONDS PAULINE LAURIN, NO. 1994.251).

TOP: Skinning a seal, Mingan, 1947 (OFFICE DU FILM DU QUÉBEC/E6, S7, P38883).

BOTTOM: Man finishing the canoe he is building, Mingan, 1947 (OFFICE DU FILM DU QUÉBEC/E6, S7, P38888).

Mingan, 1947 (OFFICE DU FILM DU QUÉBEC/E6, S7, P38889).

Damien Mestokosho and his wife building a canoe, Mingan, 1952
(WILLIAM F. STILES, NATIONAL MUSEUM OF THE AMERICAN INDIAN, GEORGE
GUSTAV HEYE CENTER. © 2004 SMITHSONIAN INSTITUTION).

The territory traveled by Mathieu Mestokosho.

FOUR

THE ABUNDANCE OF CARIBOU NEAR ATIKONAK LAKE

_____

MEETING THE INDIANS FROM SEPT-ÎLES, 1935

In the next story that I'm going to tell, I'm also going to talk about hunting and living on the land. We always took the same route to return to the land: the Saint-Jean River. This story talks about the year we hunted in the vicinity of Atikonak Lake. There was a small store there belonging to an Indian from Sept-Îles. This Indian was named Georges Jourdain.

Our group was made up of three families: my father-in-law, François Nolin, and his wife, Alice; Jérôme Napish, his wife, and his children; me and my wife and children.

We traveled up the Saint-Jean River to get to Naskaue-kan, from which we could go directly to Atikonak Lake. Long Lake is northeast of Atikonak.

At the head of Long Lake is a portage named Uapaskau. There are a lot of lakes in the area. We spent the fall there, close to the river. We slowly made our way up the river from Long Lake, waiting for the river to freeze. When it did we used our toboggans to travel up it.

We then left the river to head toward a lake near there, one we knew well. And it was near there that I noticed the "caribou steam." There must have been a lot of caribou because the cloud of steam was very big. It was very cold that morning. With our families, we approached this steam.

These were the first caribou we'd seen that year. Until then, all we'd hunted were beavers because of the snow. When we found a lake in which beavers were living, we got to work. We made holes in the ice along the shore and I'd wait for the beavers right by the dam. I was sometimes able to kill several of them. That was my job. The others had to scare them. They made holes in the ice or right in the dam itself.

As for me, I made a fire and watched for the beaver to swim to the surface. We did this work at the narrowest part of the lake, which was where the beavers built their dams. And it was there that I kept watch so I could shoot them. From time to time, I'd be warming myself by the fire when a beaver suddenly appeared. Then I had to quickly aim and fire, but I rarely missed. When there were no more beavers in the lake, we left it and found another one.

Sometimes we—the men—left the women and children at the camp and went off on our own. We took some provisions and a tent, and we stayed away for two or three days. It depended. If we saw caribou trails, we stayed longer.

That year we killed some caribou before Christmas. We killed them at a place named Kapiskauapust. We—the men— traveled with our toboggans, our provisions, and our rifles.

We knew there were caribou around there because we'd already seen the "steam." We came to the trail of four caribou and followed it. While following these caribou, we came across another trail, a much bigger one. There were many caribou in this herd, maybe twenty-five or thirty of them. But at that very moment we saw the four caribou we'd been following. One of the hunters ran after them to take position and shoot them. I hurried over and signaled to him to come back. We wanted to follow the other, more numerous caribou, so we had to abandon that small group of four. After agreeing on the plan, we set off to follow the trail of the larger herd.

The caribou changed direction. Three of them split off from the herd. It wasn't hard to follow the trail because it was December, and we could walk easily with our snowshoes. Although we hadn't seen them, we knew the caribou were nearby. They had climbed a hill and come out on a large plateau. When we came over the top of the hill, we had a clear view of the plateau; the caribou trail was wide and very visible.

We had left camp two days before and were tired. We hadn't brought a lot of provisions. We had no tobacco or tea; we'd left them at the camp for our wives. We'd brought almost nothing with us because we'd planned to be away for only a short while. But we'd already been there two days and the hunt was just starting.

When we got to the plateau and started walking across it, I said to the others that it would be better if we walked through the trees to keep out of sight. They agreed to this, saying we might be seen too soon if the herd turned back toward us. Since the wind was in our favor, the caribou would discover us only by seeing us. We began preparing: rifles, ammunition, we got everything ready. But we didn't have a clear view of the plateau because several trees blocked the view. We didn't yet know the exact location of the caribou.

Suddenly, Jérôme Napish signaled that he saw them. He was crouched down, afraid they would see him. Pointing in the direction of the herd, he indicated that I should do the same. There were some small trees there, and he wanted me to get behind them. I understood and crawled over to them. When I reached the trees, I heard the first shot. I was ready but didn't know where the caribou were; I hadn't seen a single one.

There were about thirty caribou in all. Hearing the first shot, the herd split in two. We killed twenty-six of them, and the others escaped. I managed to kill one caribou that had been wounded in the hoof. That made it twenty-seven. We had each killed several caribou.

THE ABUNDANCE OF CARIBOU NEAR ATIKONAK LAKE

As for me, I'd shot very well. I remember one big one that was fleeing and was a little too far away from me. I took a chance: I aimed carefully and managed to kill it stone dead with one bullet. When its head hit the frozen ground, a tine of its antlers broke off.

When these ones were all dead, my father-in-law asked me to go after the caribou that had escaped. But I didn't go because I was very hungry and we still had a lot of work to do on the dead caribou. Jérôme came and joined us. He told me that he had hesitated to shoot because he didn't know where I was standing in the trees, and he was afraid he might hit me by mistake. I asked him to help me bleed the caribou. I'd already done three of them. We set off together to do this job, but we didn't bleed very many because we were so hungry. We then walked over to join my father-in-law, who had made a fire and was cooking some meat. I was so tired I could barely eat. After the meal I told Jérôme that we had to cut up the caribou as soon as possible because there wasn't enough snow on the ground to cover and protect them.

That evening, we prepared a place to rest. We had to remove the snow and spread many fir and spruce boughs on the ground. We then gathered several caribou skins to use as bedding and covers. We'd been gone for three nights and had hardly slept since our departure. That night, we wanted to dry our meat. I remember that we were all very tired. But when we slept, it wasn't for long; we were sleeping under the stars, without tents and on the snow. The caribou skins and a large fire kept us warm.

We had to work during the night because we had so much to do. I built a rack while Jérôme set off to cut up a caribou we'd missed. We knew that he wouldn't be able to do this job very well, since he couldn't see much in the dark. In addition, he must have been exhausted because before we'd fixed the place to sleep we had cut up all of the caribou except that one. We had worked really hard.

It was impossible for us to transport all of the caribou bones used to make grease. So we put the meat and bones that we couldn't carry on the rack. I had an old parka with me, and I wrapped the bones in it before laying them on the rack. Finally, we wrapped everything in a tarp before covering it with fir branches. We did this because my father-in-law said that the winter would be a hard one and a lot of snow would fall on the rack.

It was the month of December, and we had finished this job. We had worked through the night. Day was breaking as we finished up. Before leaving, we ate. We still had a little tea left, but almost no tobacco. When you are in the bush and you run out of tobacco, it's terrible. We had a lot of meat but were too tired and sleepy to want to eat much.

We had left our toboggans behind so we'd make faster progress chasing the caribou. To transport all of the meat, we therefore had to use caribou skins. We wrapped the meat in the skins, and it worked pretty well. We'd chosen the largest of the caribou skins. When the meat was all tied up, we left. This was our real departure back to the camp.

It was very early in the morning. I told Jérôme that if we were too tired we'd stop along the way to make a fire and drink *tshistapakuanapui*. This involved finding some spruce boughs and boiling the cones. It didn't taste very good.

We started out. We crossed the plateau and climbed a hill. We had to walk a long way before arriving at a small river. I told Jérôme that we'd stop here to make a fire. I made the fire and he went to get water. Then, while I also went to get water, he set his kettle over the fire to boil water for spruce tea. I also had a small kettle for making tea. His was a little larger than mine. He offered me some of his tea in a cup and I drank a little. *Tshistapakuanapui* took the place of the tea that we had run out of. All you had to do to make it was gather spruce boughs and boil up the cones. Then I boiled water in my little kettle and asked Jérôme to get more water. While he was gone, I put a tiny bit of my remaining tea in the water, being careful not to waste any of the leaves. When my tea was ready, I poured in a little cold water to cool it down.

When I offered him some tea, Jérôme was surprised and happy. He said he preferred tea to the spruce drink. We talked about everything—the tea, tobacco, and flour that we had back at the camp. On this trip I had brought only two big bannocks and a little tea. I carried these provisions in a bag slung across my shoulders. This is also why we had to transport the caribou meat in the skins.

We left after drinking our tea. Just before setting off, we smoked a little tobacco. We agreed not to walk too fast.

A little farther on we came across a caribou trail. I said to Jérôme, "We'd sure have a lot of meat if we killed those caribou, too!" But we left them alone and kept going. After crossing a lake we had to climb a hill. From the top of it we could see the place where we'd slept a few nights earlier. I had to rest often; I couldn't walk fast because of the operation I'd had on my leg the year before. Jérôme got far ahead of me. I could see him in the distance, walking.

The skin that I was pulling didn't glide well over bare ice; it was easier to pull over snow. Over small branches and through bushes, it was hard. Over snow, it was fine. So, after a short rest, I continued on toward a small island where I could take another rest. Jérôme was getting farther and farther ahead of me. When I arrived at the place where, from the top of the hill, I'd spotted him, Jérôme was out of sight. The lake curved and had many islands in it, which is why I could no longer see him.

I arrived at a portage that we used in the summer. Jérôme had taken that route, and I followed his tracks. The trail came out on another lake with a stream that we had to follow. It was already dark when I arrived at the place where we'd slept. We both had very heavy loads, which completely tired us out. Arriving at another lake, I couldn't help but notice a huge beaver lodge. Then, at the end of this lake, we had to change direction. I could no longer see Jérôme. I was coming up to a plateau, and the last time I'd seen Jérôme, I'd asked him to wait for me there, and to make a fire. I was still far off when I saw him waiting for me beside his fire, which had almost gone out.

When I arrived I told him to build up the fire so we could make a good, hot drink with my few remaining tea leaves. After he rekindled the fire, and when the water was boiling, I handed him my pouch of tea. He smiled—he was glad. Our camp wasn't much farther away, and we knew that as soon as we got back we'd have some tea and tobacco as well as some bannock.

Like him, I was very glad to drink a little tea. We also ate. After the meal I rearranged my things, making sure that my ax and rifle were well tied down. We were still using the caribou skins as toboggans. I then gave Jérôme the rest of my pipe tobacco and said that this would be our last smoke before arriving back at our tents. I also asked him not to get too far ahead of me; there were a lot of hills, and we needed to help each other up them.

A little farther on we came to the trail we'd made a few days before, and after that we were able to travel a lot faster. We climbed one last hill, and upon arriving at the top, I told Jérôme he could strike out ahead of me to go light the fire in the tent. As for me, I would gather wood for it. The sky was clear and it wasn't hard to follow the trail. He started out before me. After resting a few minutes longer, I also set off.

As I approached the tent I stopped to chop a hole in the ice on the lake so we could get the water we'd need. When I finished making the hole, I headed toward our tent, still pulling my load of meat in the caribou skin.

Leaving my load near the tent, I entered it. Jérôme was already stretched out and smoking. The tent was lit by a candle. As I came in, he handed me a half-pound of tobacco. I stuffed my pipe, then lit and smoked it, sitting beside him. We were happy.

I asked him to hand me the pots so that I could go get some water. I returned with the pots full of water and, upon entering the tent, told him to bring in the caribou skins with the meat and place them along the walls of the tent. We wanted the meat to thaw.

Jérôme told me that he'd do the cooking. He fried some meat in the skillet we'd brought with us. We still had two bannocks. We ate very well. After eating we got ready to go to sleep because we were both totally exhausted. For three days we'd hardly slept at all.

When I awoke the sun was already high in the sky. I woke Jérôme so we could get ready to leave. We looked for and found our toboggans; we were glad. After eating, we folded up the tent, tied our packs onto the toboggans, and set out once again.

The load seemed different because our toboggans glided well on the snow. It was a lot easier than with the caribou skins. Jérôme and I were really happy to have our toboggans, our tea, and our tobacco.

We headed toward a lake named Kashikushit. We left a little caribou meat at this place, as well as our small stove, our pots, and several other items. We kept our rifles and the rest of the meat, as well as the caribou skins. We then headed toward the camp where our wives and children were waiting for us.

Near our camp was a lake where my father-in-law had in the past found beavers. We knew that he'd be there, along with Joseph. From a rise we had a good view of the lake, and there he was, my father-in-law, making holes in a beaver dam. Joseph was with him.

Not far away, there was another lake where Jérôme and I had set our beaver traps. My father-in-law had been visiting these traps on a regular basis for us. After joining those two on the lake, we decided to return together to the camp where our wives and children were staying, and to check the beaver traps on the way.

In our traps on the river we had some beavers. My father-in-law said, "It's not easy to kill these beavers," and, speaking directly to Joseph, he said, "Jérôme and Mathieu killed a lot of caribou." I told him we had killed a large number of caribou but at a place that was far away. We had brought back only a small amount of meat because of the great distance.

We hurried to get back to the tents, knowing that the women and my father-in-law were eager to eat some caribou. They had had nothing but beaver to eat.

The next day I again went to check my beaver traps; I had caught a big beaver. That evening we set the traps once more, since we had to leave the next day.

We all left for Kashikushit Lake, where we had left the meat, our stove, and some pots. My daughter Desneiges was born at this lake, and so we stayed there for two days. On the third day we headed toward the place where we'd killed twenty-seven caribou and where we'd seen the steam rising from a large herd of caribou. From Kashikushit Lake, we traveled in a straight line in order to pick up the trail that Jérôme and I had broken.

The story that I am now telling is still very long.

There is all of the work that we did on the twenty-seven dead caribou, and I am also going to tell you about meeting the Indians from Sept-Îles and about the arrival of the airplane that brought them provisions. The Indian from Sept-Îles was named Upikan.

At that time we stayed on the land all year round. That's why this story is so long. That year, we killed at least one hundred caribou.

These are old stories. The one I am telling you now goes back thirty years. The other story, the one about Tshishapeu from La Romaine, goes back forty years. Tshishapeu was the father of William Mark; he had come from Mingan by traveling down through the interior. I was still young at that time. But let's go back to the story I was just telling.

We had arrived at the end of Kashikushit Lake. My daughter Desneiges was born there that year. We therefore stayed at this lake for two days before setting off toward the place where we had killed a large number of caribou. The journey was longer than expected because the baby cried all the time. That slowed us down a lot. Nonetheless, by the evening of the third day, we were quite far from Kashikushit Lake. As soon as the tents were up, Jérôme left to go hunting. I loaned him my rifle because the action of his rifle was frozen. He killed four caribou very close to our camp: two females, a very small male, and a one-year-old male.

Christmas Eve was the next night.

The next morning, very early, we went to get the caribou. There were four of us. The third man was Joseph Bernard. He was still young at the time—fourteen years old—and he was about as tall as my son Marcel is today. Joseph Bernard carried back the small caribou. Jérôme and I each carried a female, and my father-in-law carried the young male. We brought them all back in one trip. It didn't take us long and wasn't too hard because Jérôme had killed them close to camp. In addition, to return to our tents, all we had to do was walk down some slopes.

When we got back we worked on the meat and the bones of the caribou. We wanted everything ready for Christmas Eve. Jérôme cracked the caribou bones to make the grease, and the women cooked the meat.

We celebrated Christmas Eve by praying to the Lord Jesus and eating caribou meat and grease.

The next morning, Christmas Day, we rested the whole day. We did the same the day after that. We ate, smoked, chatted.

On the third day, very early in the morning, we built a rack so we could leave behind some meat and equipment. Then we set off with our families on a long journey.

That evening we camped close to Kapishuapustet. The women and children stayed there; we, the men, went out later that night to prepare the trail so our move the next day would be a little easier. This scouting work led us to a small lake, and the following night we camped at this small lake. Nearby was a lake where my father-in-law found some beavers. He decided to set to work killing them. While he was doing that, I left with Joseph for an area that I knew and where I had, in the past, killed a caribou. Joseph and I returned with some meat. Then we began bringing back the meat of the twenty-seven caribou that we had already killed. We didn't have far to transport it, but it was still a big job. Even though there were several of us, we had to make three trips.

My father-in-law had no luck with those beavers. As he was checking the traps he noticed that a beaver had fled with one of his traps. While struggling and trying to force the chain, it had broken the piece of wood that was supposed to hold down the trap and the animal. The beaver then disappeared under the ice with the trap. My father-in-law had used a piece of dry wood. He knew that he'd made a mistake. Jérôme and I helped him look for that beaver, but we never found it.

One evening while we were working on the meat of our twenty-seven caribou, I managed to kill another caribou that had come right up near us on the lake. From our tents, you could see the dead caribou on the ice. I didn't bring it back right away. When I did go get it, I saw that a mink had made a hole in the snow to feed on the caribou meat. Its tracks were clearly visible in the snow. I caught that mink with a trap.

The caribou meat kept us very busy the whole time. We had to dry and smoke it. And we made a lot of grease with the bones and the marrow. The women wrapped it in bundles. We stayed there a long time in order to finish this work.

Some Indians from Sept-Îles, some hunters, came to visit us. It was Upikan, along with two other hunters, one of whom was named Edgar, the other, Charles. They spent the night with us and, that evening, we talked about hunting and their families. They didn't stay long; they left the next day. We gave them some meat. They needed it and we had a lot.

The Indians from Sept-Îles told us that they were expecting an airplane to arrive soon to replenish their supply of flour, salt, and tobacco.

After they left I set my beaver traps. I went to check them the next day and had caught two beavers. That afternoon, we packed down the trail. We were planning to take the meat with us, not to leave it on the rack.

The next day, we were ready to move our camp to another location. We traveled a long way, then set up camp close to a caribou we had killed some time before. On the site of this old camp I had left my traps and a little meat on a rack so that when I returned for the traps I'd have something to eat.

The day after the move I set some traps in this new area, but didn't go back to check them until later. That same day, I heard the sound of an airplane engine and knew that the group from Sept-Îles had received their provisions.

As for me, I returned to camp with two beavers and more meat. I'd caught four beavers in just a few days. Jérôme and my father-in-law had also killed some beavers.

The next day my father-in-law announced that the previous day, while out hunting beaver, he'd seen a caribou trail. Given the size of the trail, he thought there were several caribou in the herd. In addition, they were moving in the very direction that we wanted to go with our families, that is, toward a nearby river. So that's where we went.

The day after the move, four of us men left to follow the caribou trail: my father-in-law, Jérôme, Joseph, and me. It was a long walk. Near the river we decided not to walk in the open on the ice, but instead to remain in the trees so the caribou wouldn't see us. When we caught up with them they were on the river—out in the open. We split into twos to hunt them. We knew that the caribou would scatter in all directions. But within two days we had killed twelve caribou and returned home. The whole camp then moved to near the place where we'd killed the caribou.

There were a lot of caribou in the area, and my father-in-law knew that. Rather than work on the ones we had killed, we set out once again to go hunting. My father-in-law found the trail of a big herd—more than thirty caribou. We followed this trail, which was very wide. The caribou were headed toward open ground. Jérôme spotted them far off in the hills. But the caribou had seen us and fled. The three other hunters chased them while I stayed behind to wait for the animals that would retrace their steps. Jérôme and the others succeeded in killing twelve caribou during their chase.

I just waited, huddled between two trees. After some time, five caribou suddenly appeared on the trail. I succeeded in killing all of them. I was alone. I then moved the dead caribou to a place well sheltered from the wind so I could work on the meat. I didn't even stop to make a fire. I waited there for the other hunters to return, and they arrived that evening. The days were starting to get longer; it was February. By the time the others arrived, I had finished my work. All of the meat was nicely cut and buried in the snow. I had killed four adult caribou and one small animal in its first year.

Before setting out for home, we made a fire so we could eat. In just a few days we had killed about thirty caribou. That year, I'm pretty sure we killed about one hundred caribou.

We had a lot of meat and a lot of work. We didn't know what we were going to do with all the surplus meat. My father-in-law asked us to go to Tshiask Lake, which was in the area where I'd heard the sound of the airplane engine. We were going there to find the other Indians, the ones from Sept-Îles. Earlier in the winter they had told Jérôme that they'd be camping at Tshiask Lake at the end of February. I was very familiar with this lake and had no trouble finding it.

Tshiask Lake is not very deep. Even in summer, it dries up in certain places. Upikan had told Jérôme that he would camp at a place where it would be easy to get water; that is, where the lake was deep enough. So we headed toward the end of the lake. There was so little water in the lake that, while out on the ice, it seemed like we were walking on a plain.

I spotted their camp at the end of the lake. There was only one tent but it was a big one. Nine people were living in it. The men had arrived the day before with the flour and other provisions that they had picked up at Natuaiau, on Atikonak Lake. They had two log cabins in that area, near the falls on Atikonak Lake. Three of them had traveled there to pick up the provisions. We saw the three toboggans they'd used. They were running a little low on tea, but had a good supply of flour, salt, and tobacco.

They invited us into their tent. For dinner they offered us meat and macaroni. They had killed seven caribou in the last few days. When we finished eating, they cleared a place in the tent for us to sleep.

The next day it snowed. My friend Upikan said to me, "You can stay another night if you want." But I replied, "We have to leave today, my friend, because my father-in-law asked me to bring him back some tea as soon as possible. That's what our father-in-law especially wanted."

He agreed. I asked him for some pipe tobacco as well as cigarette tobacco. He replied that they didn't have much tobacco. All they had was one can of pipe tobacco, and it was a small can. The plane had brought only cigarette tobacco, although they had asked for pipe tobacco.

In the end he gave us eight pouches of cigarette tobacco, just one box of salt, and three pounds of tea. It wasn't much but it was better than nothing. We were especially short of tea. We paid for these provisions. In addition, Upikan gave me a half-box of salt. He said he'd been keeping it for his brother-in-law, whose nickname was Pess.

Jérôme already had a toboggan, and Upikan loaned me one. On the return trip Jérôme was carrying one bag of flour, candles, and the pots. I was carrying one pot of grease, some macaroni, and the salt, tea, and tobacco.

Our camp was a one-day walk away. We had to cross a long plateau, then a lake. On the other side of this lake, in the trees, we stopped to make a fire and eat. We had stopped to eat at the same place while traveling to Tshiask Lake. Our teakettles were right where we'd left them. We arrived back home late that night.

Everyone in camp was happy to see us because they were eager to eat bannock and caribou stew. We had a really good meal that night.

We were supposed to meet Upikan at his log cabin, at Natuaiau on Atikonak Lake, a few days later. We had decided this as we were saying goodbye to him that morning. So, four days later, as soon as the snow was good for snowshoeing, we returned to Atikonak Lake. Upikan had arrived at his cabin the day before. He was with his fiancée, Marie-Louise.

When I got there he was inside with her. He was sitting beside her, repairing his snowshoes. His sister and brother-in-law, the brother of his fiancée, had come with them, but they were out checking their traps for muskrat when we arrived. Upikan's brother-in-law was named Paul-Aimé.

Upikan was alone in the cabin with Marie-Louise, and I think we disturbed them, the lovers. But they had done some cooking and offered us a good meal. They looked after us very well. By the time we finished eating, it was dark.

Jérôme and I went to bed. The cabin had two rooms. The floor of ours was covered with spruce boughs, but in the room where the others slept there were beds.

The next day we ate again, then chose the provisions that we wanted. When we were ready, and as we were leaving the house, Upikan said, "We are also leaving. Tomorrow, it'll be our turn to visit you."

I was still with Jérôme. We started toward home. After walking a long time we stopped at the place where we'd left our teakettles, to make a fire and drink some tea. It was close to a river that looked like a plain.

That evening, when we arrived home, I said to my father-in-law, "We must get ready; we're going to have visitors." We had a large quantity of grease and caribou meat. We also had a good supply of beaver meat.

The next day, at noon, the children saw them headed down the lake. Coming to visit us meant a long detour for them. They were returning to their respective camps, to rejoin the other Indians from Sept-Îles. They left our tents that evening, not stopping to spend the night with us.

Their journey was a long one. They'd come all the way from the falls at Atikonak Lake and were headed to Tshiask Lake, where the other Indians were waiting for them.

Upikan told us he'd left a message in his cabin for the pilot of the plane, in case he returned. In the message he'd asked for more pipe tobacco, or that's what he said during his visit with us.

It was a very nice day. My father-in-law said to him, "We're also leaving. We'll be on our way as soon as we finish drying and smoking the caribou meat."

My wife asked one of the men with Upikan for some thread.

Edgar and Tipak, Upikan's sons, planned to hunt beaver for a few days near the end of Tshiask Lake. Then, after checking their traps, they decided to visit us again. They thought we'd still be at the same place, but we'd left two days earlier. Our new camp was far away.

Edgar and Tipak followed our tracks, walking a long distance. They arrived in the evening at the camp we had left that morning. They had a big dog with them. Edgar said to Tipak, "It will soon be night but we can't turn back now. We have to follow their trail. They can't have gone very far because they are transporting so much." And they started walking once again. It was already dark. They crossed a river and climbed a small mountain; they were following the trail we'd made in the morning. Much later, they came to the small lake where we were camped. Out tents had been up for a long time when they arrived. They were exhausted. They spent the rest of the night with us and left the next morning.

We also left—just the men, who had to pack the trail. It was essential that we prepare the trail because we had such a big load of meat. We headed toward Mistiskuateu or Mistiskuatiku Lake, I can't quite remember its name.

The next day we took this trail with the women, children, and all of our packs. At the end of this move, once our camp was well organized, I went back to the area we had just left. I returned to the place where my father-in-law lost the beaver that had escaped with one of his traps. Nearby was a big mountain, and I climbed it. It was very cold and I was freezing, even though I was fat and well clothed. From up there I scanned the countryside in every direction. I could clearly pick out, in the snow, lower down on a plateau, the biggest caribou trail that I'd ever seen. There were really a lot of caribou in the area that winter. That trail must have been fifteen feet wide.

I returned home to tell my father-in-law what I'd seen. When he heard this, he said, "We're not hungry. We must not disturb these caribou. Instead, we'll hunt beaver and then move to other places."

So we split up for a few days. I went with my family in one direction, Jérôme headed in another direction. My father-in-law ended up at a lake where he found some beavers. Since there were quite a few of them, Jérôme joined him there. They found three beaver lodges.

I was also hunting beaver, and I quickly located a lodge. I killed all of the beavers in it, with the exception of a small one that escaped. I then went back and camped on the river that flowed into the lake where Jérôme and my father-in-law were hunting.

Jérôme came to see me, saying, "You're so lucky. You've already killed your beavers, but we're still working hard to kill ours." Then he said, "I saw the caribou whose trail you spotted a few days ago. It's a very large herd. I didn't hunt them, since we have enough meat. But I really wanted to go see them. Just as you said, that trail is very large."

The next day I left the river and set out to join my family, who were camped near one of the old racks where we kept our surplus meat. That's where we were all supposed to meet, my family and the others. That was where we'd spent Christmas. But it was then the month of March and spring was on its way.

So, carrying some meat from our rack, as well as more than the usual number of packs, we set out. We didn't progress very rapidly because of the packs and the young children who couldn't yet walk. This time we were leaving for good; our destination: Lake Brûlé.

We traveled every day without once stopping to hunt. We made it all the way to Lake Brûlé traveling like that. We didn't meet any other Indians along the way.

Later, we arrived at Maskuekan. A little farther on, at a place named Kanetinat, we did meet some other Indians: the late Damien Napish, Étienne Louis, Bastien Louis, and Antoine Napish. There were a lot of children. Étienne had already married, but not Antoine. All of them were from Mingan.

Damien gave us some salt. We were happy to see them. We gave them some meat and, as you know, we had a lot to share.

Finally, we left for Mingan, traveling every day. That year we arrived in Mingan at the end of April.

This is where my story ends.

PART TWO

FIVE

REFLECTIONS ON THE **SO-CALLED** **LAZINESS** OF INDIANS

PREJUDICES RELATED TO HARDSHIP AND IGNORANCE

There are some people who say that the Indians don't hunt enough when they are out on the land and that they spend all of their time asleep in their tents. The merchants and missionaries say this; I've heard them time and time again. I think that they're wrong and they're not speaking the truth.

I've seen the Elders and listened to their stories of the hunt. I've hunted my entire life, and it was by hunting that I was able to live.

In the old days, some Indians didn't manage to survive. Entire families experienced great hardship. They desperately tried to stay alive. They were starving. The hunters searched everywhere for caribou but didn't find any. There was nothing more they could do.

As history tells it, the previous winter, these families had killed a lot of caribou. They had killed too many of them. The young hunters had chased the caribou until the entire herd fell into the ravine at Churchill Falls. These people were crazy; they made fun of the caribou.

The following year they didn't find any caribou. The families decided to head back down to Mingan but they encountered all sorts of problems. They didn't kill anything. They were all very weak. They could barely walk because their legs and arms hurt and they were freezing cold. From time to time, a hunter killed a porcupine or a grouse. But that was all. And they could never find a place to make a fire rock when they stopped to camp at night. Some of them died along the way.

In winter, in the woods, when it's extremely cold, it can seem like the forest is a desert. There are no porcupines, no grouse, and the caribou are hard to find. So the hunter looks for a rock under the snow with which to make a fire. When he finds one, he digs a hole in the snow to expose the rock and the surrounding ground. He then makes a fire out of green wood right on the rock, which is in the middle of the hole. All around it, hunters lay down fir boughs to make a floor. Then, around the hole, they plant poles to serve as walls and, over them, lay a canvas tarp.

In the center of this, you continue heating up the rock. In the beginning, you have to make sure that the coals stay on the rock and don't slip to the side. When the rock is nice and warm, you hit it with sticks to chip it and even it out. You also stuff green wood under it so that it heats up all over. Then you hit it on the bottom to flatten it out. This worked best when the rock was surrounded by sand. If the hunters succeeded in making a good fire rock, the families stayed warm. But they still didn't have anything to eat. Sitting around that rock, they were warm, but they were still hungry.

The colder it is, the harder it is to hunt. A hunter who is walking a lot and doesn't eat is always cold. He can barely walk. He has no more marrow in his bones. And yet he must keep walking because he is not finding anything. These hunters have sore knees, they have trouble getting their legs to bend, and they become very weak. But they must keep on hunting.

In winter, when the lakes are frozen, you still have to find and kill fish. You have to break the ice along a line of the right length, set the nets in the water, and catch the lake trout or other fish. You also have to fish through the ice using a hook—chop a hole at a place where you know there are fish. Even if the ice is as thick as two lengths of stovepipe, you still have to fish. You have to break the ice, then slide the net into the water. You attach the net to a rope that goes under the ice. At each end the rope is tied to poles set in the ice. The net is under the ice, attached to the rope by pieces of wood.

When there is nothing else to eat you have to catch fish. They are the last hope for food. At night the hunter goes and tugs on the rope the net is attached to. If he senses fish in the net, he pulls it in and takes the catch back to the tent.

Then, at last, the starving hunter can eat. It wasn't easy, but that's the way it was.

Despite all that, the whites still say that the Indians were not good hunters. Take, for example, the wife of one of the merchants in Mingan, John's late wife, who criticized us so much. She complained to the missionary about how lazy Indians were. She claimed that Indians only hunted to survive and that, as soon as they had what they needed, they took it easy, they slept. But Indians almost never stopped hunting. They had no choice.

We hunted for food but we also hunted animals for their furs.

From time to time, a hunter had to watch as one of his children died from hunger out on the land. And he felt great sorrow when that happened. But he was living on the land to work. He had no choice. And he worked very hard so that everything would be alright.

You traveled constantly when you were living on the land. Sometimes, the cold was almost unbearable. When it was really cold, no one could relax.

When a hunter spotted a caribou trail, he had to follow it, find the caribou, and kill them. Even if he has killed caribou, the hunter must keep hunting because a supply of meat doesn't last long. There are children and old people to feed.

Let's say three hunters kill six caribou. Each family therefore gets two caribou. With two caribou, a family has food for several days. You eat all of the bone fat from the caribou. That's what makes you strong. Caribou bone marrow is particularly rich and nourishing for the hunter and his family.

After a period when you don't eat, you mustn't eat too much caribou. This meat is very strong, and anyone who hasn't eaten it for some time will suffer if he eats too much. He becomes very weak, he feels heavy, he can feel the effect of the food in his blood. He spends the whole day stretched out. The next day, he is fine.

Yes, that's what it's like on the land.

I saw whites at Lake Brûlé who died. I saw more than one of them, at this lake and even farther away. They didn't die from hunger, since they always had bannock to eat. They died from illness.

I remember there were two white trappers and one of them got sick and died. The other one, who was alone, starved and eventually died. Often, whites don't know how to hunt. They trap for furs and, for the most part, eat their provisions. They don't hunt for their food. This white man, when he found himself alone, didn't know how to hunt and he ran out of provisions. Given his situation, he was bound to die.

Indians don't have this type of problem. They are never alone. They supported each other a lot. If one Indian was too weak, someone else hunted for him and his family.

We took turns hunting during periods of hardship. Until no one could walk anymore. As far as I know that happened only once, a long time ago. Never, during my life, have I seen or heard of a whole family starving to death. Some people die from not getting enough to eat. But families make it through in the end.

The Elders used to say something else about helping one another. Sometimes, a man will hunt a lot, while his companion takes it easy. The latter doesn't go hunting, thinking that the other one will give him something to eat when he has killed a lot of game. The person who thinks this pretends to hunt but is really hiding in the woods, close to the camp. Yes, there are hunters who've done that.

If the hunters don't find caribou, they hunt for porcupines at night, near their tents. If they kill some porcupines, three or four of them, then everyone is happy. The women make a fire to remove the porcupine quills and everyone eats. But food is scarce, and these porcupines are not enough. The next day you have to hunt all the more. In times of hardship, ruffed grouse are wary. They fly off quickly—always too quickly for the hunter. Then you must move the tents, change location, because hunters must be forever on the move in order to get lucky and kill animals.

In the old days it was always a big job to set up a good camp in winter. You had to find a promising spot and dig out a fire rock from under a thick layer of snow. Sometimes, it was hard to find.

How courageous and hardworking they were, the Elders!

Today there are stoves. All you have to do is place the stove on four feet. But the fire rock heated a tent very well. When you had a good fire rock, it was better than a stove. You had to protect the smoke hole at the top of the tent by placing a tarp up against the wind. That way, the smoke didn't come back into the tent. There was never a lot of smoke in the tents. There was a little but not too much.

If the camp is well set up, if a caribou has been killed, then the hunter hunts for money, especially for marten. He sets traps all over, sometimes far away from the camp and during cold spells. There is a lot of snow. All of the animals live under the snow. During cold spells they don't go out. Neither do the hunters go out. Yes, it was like that.

Occasionally, you hear that someone has no luck hunting. Anyone who never has luck doesn't watch over his traps or travel enough. The one who works hard always ends up killing something. He finds his luck again. But you have to hunt constantly to have good luck.

In my case, I worked very hard. I've always worked hard and still do. Those I hunted with, they were all hardworking, all good hunters. We never stopped, and luck was on our side. We set our traps far away from our tents, but we always caught animals. And if luck was really on our side we would kill some caribou while out setting our traps. At times like that we didn't travel as much. We stayed longer in one place. And we trapped martens.

There's one thing I want to say. The Indians from Mingan do not hunt fox. We have always killed caribou, beaver, and marten. But we didn't hunt foxes that much. I've killed only a few in my life. The Indians who spent the winter close to Mingan, those ones killed more foxes than we did. But they still didn't kill a lot of them. It was considered good if a family killed four foxes over the entire winter. Fox was worth a lot, but we didn't like to hunt it. People from Mingan were all like that.

I always say that the work done by Indians on the land was hard work. But we did this work as best we could. Those of my generation liked to hunt, liked our work.

Transporting provisions, that was hard. Being able to withstand the cold, that was hard. Still, the hardest part was continuing to hunt in periods of famine. During those times the hunter did everything possible to hold on until spring. Because in spring it wasn't the same at all; it was easier to find food.

You could find fish easily in spring. Ice on the lake was no longer a problem. The lake trout were fat and good to eat. And to stay fit you needed to eat some of them.

Hunters regularly left the women and children at the camp. They'd leave for several days, head to some faraway spot. We never went alone. If there were four hunters in the group, we set off in pairs.

On occasion we slept under the stars, in winter, with a campfire keeping us warm. But usually, during these hunting trips, we set up a small tent at night. There was smoke in these tents. That's the reason why I now have trouble with my eyes; I'm almost blind. All the very old people who lived on the land had bad eyes.

You must never waste caribou meat. Whatever cannot be eaten right away must be stored. We smoked the meat and placed it on racks in well-sheltered places. We had racks in all the places we thought we'd be during the winter. You had to foresee these things. If caribou could not be found, you hunted other animals and tried to hold on until spring. There were winters like that, with no caribou.

Today, we live among the whites. There are snowmobiles. We're already getting them ready for the coming winter. The Indians will use their snowmobiles to go hunting this winter. But I learned that real hunting must be done in the silence. A good caribou hunter makes no noise. Snowmobiles make noise. You can't hunt caribou in a snowmobile.

In the old days no one slept rather than go hunting. The merchants and missionaries were telling big lies. These days, I can no longer hunt. I'll never hunt again. But I'm proud of what I did, of my work on the land. I never slept more than necessary. The money I receive today for doing nothing is owed to me because I worked my entire life. Now, it's up to the government to support me, since it can do that.

On the land we would all have died if we hadn't had fish. We always had lake trout in with our other provisions when we traveled. There was always fish to help us, in addition to porcupine.

The best region for hunting porcupines was north of Winuakapau Lake. We knew there were a lot of porcupines there; despite that, they weren't always easy to find. When everything is covered with snow, it's hard to kill porcupines, even if they are plentiful.

I hunted porcupines in that area. In winter, I'd go there with Peter Piétasho, Damien, and Sylvestre. We shared the work. Damien and Sylvestre broke the trail that we would take later on. Peter and I, we hunted the porcupines. We teased each other, always trying to kill more porcupines than the other person so you could make fun of him. We always hunted "little necks" (porcupines). We'd leave camp together, then split up for a few hours. Porcupines usually live along small streams. That's where I most often hunted them, in deserted places near small waterways.

That time I was with Peter, who was off hunting on his own, I easily killed four porcupines. I was glad my luck was so good. Porcupines were plentiful in the area where I was hunting. There were porcupine tracks everywhere. So I returned to camp with my four porcupines.

Peter hadn't killed anything. The women were preparing the meal. Porcupine is delicious to eat, you know. I, along with everyone else, was glad about that hunt. But Peter really wanted to kill some porcupines. He said, "I spoke to the others. Instead of traveling tomorrow we want to go hunt porcupines, each on our own." We all agreed. We wanted this meat because it's very good to eat. And Peter wanted another chance to tease me.

I hadn't told anyone that I'd seen all of those porcupine tracks, and I returned to the same place as before, easily killing two porcupines. But that day I was even luckier with grouse. As I was hunting for porcupines, I killed seven grouse.

I was the first to return to camp. On the trail home, walking with my catch on my back, I said to myself that everything was going well for us. I wondered if Peter had killed any porcupines. He returned early in the evening with the others. They were smiling. Peter had three porcupines; Damien, two; and Sylvestre, one. The women were very glad. We had brought back good food for the children. To tell the truth, that winter we had as much as we needed. Game animals were plentiful and luck was on our side.

We were very close to North West River and decided to go stay there for a while. We stayed mainly around Kakatshu-Uatshistun.

Yes, that's how we hunted in my time. There wasn't constant hardship. We knew how to hunt and we succeeded in finding food. Today, the ways of the whites are taking over. We trap fur-bearing animals but don't go out on the land to find our food. We take our provisions with us.

I've known white hunters. In my time, there were a lot of them living in the bush, especially around North West River and around here, near the ocean. These hunters took huge quantities of provisions with them. They lived in log cabins. It's amazing how much flour they'd have stored away. We'd visit these white hunters and, as we entered their cabins, they'd hide their flour. But they always asked us for meat. They especially wanted caribou.

Like us, they hunted fur-bearing animals, but they didn't know how to kill caribou. They didn't hunt their food on the land, and they always told us that they never saw any caribou. They were alone and didn't travel far.

We, however, were never alone. We often went out hunting beaver with the women. We traveled constantly. Even when we had ample provisions, we didn't stop hunting. We were always trying to find caribou because we always wanted to know where they were.

When the men left to hunt caribou, the women, the children, and the old people stayed at the camp.

From time to time, there would be a large group of us out hunting caribou. If a large herd had gathered on a lake for several days, many hunters learned about it or simply seemed to know. As I said, we always tried to know where the caribou were heading. Thus, there might be a group of eight or ten men from different camps out to hunt the same herd. Sometimes, when we hunted caribou, we'd be a two- or three-day walk away from our camp. It was the same for the others. In one day we could cover a great distance on foot, since we weren't carrying packs.

Yes, it was like that.

I remember one day when there were eight of us hunters. We killed thirty caribou. To do this, we had waited for the caribou to pass by a place we'd decided upon, since we always bled the dead animals before covering them with snow. Then each group returned to its camp, and everyone moved close to the place where we'd killed the caribou. At that point, everyone got to work: the hunters, the women, the old, and the young.

When the meat was well protected and placed on the racks, we stayed at that place for several weeks. To pass the time the young people learned how to hunt fur-bearing animals.

We were once again close to North West River and so we decided to go there. We were short of flour. At that time, the camp was made up of six families. We had the meat of thirty-six caribou to help us through. As for the flour, we'd soon be in North West River. We stayed in our camp for three weeks, making sure our meat was well taken care of. We left on New Year's Day.

We traveled down the Hamilton River in the direction of North West River. Everything was going well for us. The six families had as much food as they could eat.

But not everyone was as lucky as we were. On the way to North West River we met some Indians from Mingan. They were hungry, that group. Joachim Pawstuk's father was with them. He had suffered the most. The others were still walking without problem, but his face was frostbitten. He refused to eat meat. Like the whites, all he wanted to eat was flour, bannock. That group was also headed toward North West River.

Hunters set their traps for fur-bearing animals mostly at night. During the day, we often traveled or tried to locate the caribou. Once the tent was set up and the camp all arranged, the hunter would go put out his traps. Or sometimes he had to go back a long way to check the traps he'd set near an old campsite. In that case, he often went alone, without a big pack, trying to walk as fast as possible. If luck was with him, he killed two or three marten for every five traps.

Setting up tents, hunting, walking all the time—it was a lot of work. Sometimes the snow would not support our weight, and walking became very difficult. Breaking trail was particularly tiring. But, you see, the merchants didn't believe all of that. They weren't out there with us.

I'd like to have seen the merchants that I knew do the work I did on the land. These merchants would never have been able to go where I went. Even without packs, they would never have been able to follow me out on the land.

Perhaps you've heard this story. There were two white trappers working out on the land close to Mingan. One was named Michaud; I can't remember the name of the other one. They ran out of provisions. It was winter and they probably couldn't get back to Mingan. To survive, they ate their candles.

That's why I don't like it when people tell stories about how lazy and destitute the Indians were out on the land. The whites found it harder than we did. It wasn't their work. They trapped but didn't know how to hunt. To each his own work. Out on the land the whites worry all the time and wear themselves out for nothing. Walking tires them out. They're not at home.

It's the opposite for the Indians. They're at home. They know how to hunt, and they never stop hunting.

It was hard, but we made it, on our own. We were proud of this work, of our hunting.

SIX

DAILY LIFE ON THE LAND

COMMENTS ON THE SKILLS
AND PERSEVERANCE OF MEN AND WOMEN

The women also worked a lot. They set snares to trap rabbits, they caught fish, they hunted porcupines, looked after the children and old people, made the food, kept a careful watch over the fire, and made sure there was firewood on hand. They did a lot of other things, as well. Like us, the women never stopped working.

When a camp was newly set up, the hunters went with the women to set snares. They left early in the morning and walked a distance equivalent to a two-day walk with packs. Together, they set out several snares, returning to the camp that evening. Then, while the men were far off somewhere hunting, the women checked their snares.

When their husbands were hunting big game, it was also hunting season for the women, because they did more than just hunt for rabbits. They put out traps for marten. They killed a lot of animals and brought back good food.

The checking of the snares took almost a whole day. The women went in pairs to do that. On occasion, they also took the children. If they arrived back at the camp early enough, they went and checked the nets on the lake. If the lakes were not yet frozen, they had several nets to check.

They had to bring in the fish, carefully set out the nets again—there were often three nets to a lake—and return to camp with their catch.

They cleaned the fish, cutting them in two pieces, lengthwise, so that they could be dried and smoked. When that was done they removed the fish from the fire and wrapped them in birch bark. These birch bark rolls were then wrapped in canvas and placed by the women on racks, up out of the reach of the dogs.

The women always took the same trails. They were very skilled with rifles and shotguns. Depending on the situation, they hunted the same way the men did. All of the women knew how to shoot. Some of them were really good at it; they could kill any animal. But because of their work, they didn't go very far from the camp. With the help of the dogs, they often killed porcupines.

Sometimes, the hunters left the women on their own for a month or longer. They managed. We didn't worry at all about leaving the women at the camp. But, as a precaution, we never left for long periods without first ensuring that the women had a good supply of meat. You couldn't forget the children: sometimes there were a lot of them. Without a supply of meat, the women wouldn't have been able to feed them. No family lives on bannock alone.

If the women had not routinely killed porcupines, rabbits, and fish, no one would have survived out on the land. Some families experienced great hardship because they had too many children. I was in that situation a couple of times. Without what the women caught, we wouldn't have managed.

Normally, we left the women alone at the camp for a week. When we traveled far away we were hunting caribou. If luck was with us we killed several animals. Then, all we did was bleed them and cover them with snow. We cut off only a few pieces of fresh meat so we could quickly return to the camp with them. We got back as soon as possible to announce the good news to the women.

The next day, or even the day after, we all moved near the place where the caribou hunt had taken place. Sometimes we even transported the provisions we had placed on our racks. A big move like this could involve up to one week's work. We transported the provisions from the racks only if we were sure we would not pass by there again.

Yes, that's how it was. We all knew where we were and where we were going. We knew every bit of the country and the names of all the lakes, all the trails. We had racks everywhere along our route, all along the route we intended to follow there and back. We knew exactly where these racks were and the amount and quality of the provisions stored on each one. There were racks with caribou meat, racks with fish. There were still others with porcupines, with rabbits, and with grouse. There were even some on which we'd hidden bear meat.

All of these provisions were very carefully wrapped. A good hunter never lost his surplus meat due to spoilage.

When caribou were killed, the first thing we ate was the heads. They were roasted, turning on a rope over the fire. That was delicious. We stayed with the women at such times; we had to help prepare the meat. In addition, the women would tell us if they'd seen any beaver lodges while out checking their snares. If they had, we went and killed the beavers.

We saw a lot of game early in the winter, when the lakes were starting to freeze. By examining the tracks in the snow, we could get an idea of the number of caribou and in what directions they had gone. We also set many traps for fur-bearing animals at that time of year.

While doing that we were breaking trail for later; we packed the snow beforehand along the route we'd soon be traveling with our packs and our families.

We set out in pairs to lay traps in various directions. We were especially interested in finding marten and mink.

We made traps out of wood. It took us longer, but these traps were more efficient. I did a lot of trapping with wooden traps. I knew how the Elders had done it, since it was they who had shown me how. The other hunters with me also knew how. Steel traps are good, but they're heavy if you have a lot to transport. We worked hard and liked to set as many traps as possible. When we wanted more traps, we'd make wooden ones right on the spot, just as we'd learned. It took us two or three days to do this work.

In my time we ate marten. The women boiled it until the meat fell off the bones.

The men and the women worked together on the skins of the fur-bearing animals that we caught in our traps.

We made toboggans out of wood at the start of winter. It was the men who did that, during their first long journey to set traps and locate the caribou. We set these traps far away, always in the direction we had to go with our families.

When there was enough snow on the ground and our traps were set, we returned to the family camp pulling our toboggans, which were loaded with our first kill of the season. Back at the men's camp, from where we had just come, we'd left provisions on our racks. We'd also left equipment, all sorts of things—our snowshoes, for example, in case we needed them later on, when we arrived with our families.

As we were walking back home, we knew that the women had been hunting while we were away. The racks at the family camp would be stacked high with fish, rabbits, and porcupines. We knew that the women had managed fine on their own.

When we arrived back we took over the hunting around the camp. It was important not to use up the stored food too quickly, and we needed fresh food for the coming days, when we'd be traveling.

Before the first major move the men made snowshoe frames, while the women made straps from dried skins and also *babiche* for the webbing. We repaired old snowshoes and made new ones.

If there were sufficient provisions at the camp, we'd decide to leave our families once again and set out on another long journey to check our traps. We took our toboggans and our snowshoes because it was the season for snow, even if the very cold weather had not yet arrived.

We used to trap a lot of marten. Once, after checking my trap line, I returned with eight or ten marten. We also trapped weasel, mink, and otter.

A good way to catch otter was to find an abandoned beaver dam. In the gap where the stream flowed, the trapper could set a trap underwater. Then, if the stream wasn't too wide, the otter had to swim right past the trap.

We caught a lot of fur-bearing animals at that time of year. There would be snow on the ground but it wasn't too cold. So the animals were out and about and we were able to catch them. While we were taking care of our traps, we watched for caribou. Later on, when it got really cold, we would have to spend less time on our traps and more time hunting caribou. As for the traps, we had to make sure they didn't disappear under a thick blanket of snow.

After a while we returned to the family camp in order to move it. While traveling between the hunters' camp and the family camp, we counted all the beaver lodges, intending to kill these beavers as soon as the family camp was moved and set up farther along. After transporting and setting up the camp, we went back and killed those beavers. We also walked ahead some distance to reset the traps that hadn't caught anything where they'd been set before. And we walked in all directions to find out where the caribou were.

As you see, we Indians, we worked. There was always something to do, even when we were spending a few days at the camp with our families.

Some evenings we stretched out in the tent with the women and children. We rested a little. But the next day, before sunrise, we were back at work again. At home, we helped the women gather firewood and made the rounds of their snares. Because the women had a lot to do.

They cooked the food, repaired the clothes, boiled them to wash them, and took care of the children and old people. They cleaned the animal skins and, in addition, hunted and fished. They never stopped, and often didn't even have time to eat the food they needed.

The hunters might stay with their families for periods of one week. Then they left again, set off on their own, always to a more distant place to reset their traps and check new areas. If these were rich in game, the family camp was moved to the hunting grounds, while the hunting camps were relocated farther along.

It was always like that. The men always tried to check their traps in the evening, even after having moved camp during the day. All of the hunters worked a lot.

Occasionally, we moved things well ahead of time to a future campsite. In particular, we moved the surplus provisions from our racks.

The men hunted caribou when they had time. They set out in pairs in all directions. You had to count on your luck. Believe me, some hunters were very lucky. They were always in the right spot. Others, however, never found caribou. They'd have died if they'd been alone. But any meat that we brought home was shared.

All of this work and this moving around were very tiring. Some Indians became demoralized and started to waste food or to hunt as little as possible. The hardest part was transporting provisions. When we had to move a lot of caribou meat in addition to our packs, it tired everyone out.

There were even some who abandoned meat or packs on their racks. They left them there and never returned for them. Becoming discouraged and forgetting about surplus meat was a serious mistake. You always had to take precautions to avoid starvation.

With the family and the packs, you covered about eight miles a day. When you moved the family camp, it was to set it up a two-day walk from where it had been. You always stopped at the end of the afternoon, since you had to set up the tents quite early if you wanted to go hunting and break trail for the next day. Upon arriving at a new campsite, the women were responsible for gathering a supply of firewood. They worked at that in the early evening.

Sheet-metal stoves heated our tents. We were lucky if, every evening after arriving at a new campsite, the hunters came back with porcupines and grouse.

When he wasn't going too far away, the hunter took his young son along. The boy followed his father, carrying a small-caliber rifle. He listened to what his father was teaching him and practiced his aim while trying to shoot grouse with his gun.

That's what it was like when everything was going well. You kept the flour for the infants. The women made them grouse stew. The rest of the family ate meat.

Out on the land, as I've often said, it was better not to depend on your supply of flour. Anyone who did so was making a mistake; it was a sure sign of future famine and hardship. It was the hunt that provided our food. You always had to keep in mind that you might fall on hard times. So you had to hunt constantly to have a reserve of meat.

Flour was not as important as fish, believe me. In winter, fishing demanded a lot of effort and work. The ice was sometimes so thick that all of the men had to work together to set a net. Then, we had to move the net regularly to improve our chances of catching something. Each time, it was a tough job to break the ice. Even in winter we sometimes had three nets out at a time, like in the fall. In addition to these nets, we chopped holes in the ice so we could fish for trout using hooks. We thought about only one thing: making sure we had a good supply of food.

You see how hard it was. We were full of spirit. All those who say the Indians didn't know how to do anything, they're big liars. I know what I'm talking about, and I knew the Elders. The merchants and priests lied about us, I tell you. They never knew what we did at our camps, out on the land, to survive. You had to be strong and spirited, and we were proud of what we accomplished.

When we had everything we needed and game was plentiful, we stayed in one area. That's when the hunters spent more time trapping fur-bearing animals.

Some families were unlucky. I knew of some young hunters who didn't help the old people enough. These young men were afraid to walk a lot. They wanted to stay in camp, so they'd pretend they were gathering firewood. But it's the women who've done that from the beginning of time. Young men who refused to hunt caused great harm to their families out on the land. Because if a young hunter doesn't hunt, he brings on hardship. These young people should have helped their parents and worked constantly to bring back good food. A neglectful young hunter worked a lot less than a woman. In addition, she was a better hunter than him. Because the women hunted a lot. They did all the work around camp and then went out hunting. Not only did they set snares, they also brought in a lot of furs. Yes, the women were very good hunters. They really knew how to set a snare.

It was in mid-December, upon the arrival of the intense cold, that the work eased a bit. But you had to have a good supply of food by then. That was also when the hunters tried to kill caribou. There was a pretty good chance of killing caribou in December.

To make a good meal, you need grease. We obtained grease for when we ate rabbit by killing caribou. Many edible animals don't have enough fat on them to make grease.

We always kept the lard from the store in reserve for times when we failed to kill caribou. But some Indians couldn't resist the temptation and started making their meals with store-bought lard in the fall. Come winter, they'd have run out.

Grease is important to a meal. It's the reason we loved to kill caribou, beavers, and porcupines. So you didn't have to depend on the provisions from the store or from others. You had to hunt!

You'd often hear certain Indians say, "That guy had a lot of salt and wouldn't give me any. This one had a huge supply of flour and he kept it all to himself." That wasn't exactly true. Indians shared meat and provisions; normally, people didn't refuse anything at all to a visitor. But eventually we all got to know each other. And occasionally we knew that a visitor who'd come to ask for flour was one of those who preferred to eat bannock rather than meat. So he wasn't asking for flour for his baby or because he was down on his luck; he needed flour because he wasted it. He ate too much flour and didn't hunt enough.

There were always Indians like that. There were some at the time of the Elders, there were some on the land when I was still hunting, and there are some right here in the village.

But let's get back to our story. It was now the month of January. There was a thick blanket of snow on the ground. We were living mainly off our provisions from the previous month, when the hunting was good. In January, the caribou move around a lot and it's the best time to see their tracks. The men would hunt. We would head toward Katshimitat-sishkat, an area known for caribou. We covered a short distance every day; we were looking for caribou tracks.

When we stopped in the evening to camp, the old men hunted for porcupines and the rest of us for caribou. If we found some caribou, we didn't kill them right away, that night. Instead, we returned to the tent to announce the good news to the others. In the case of caribou, the more hunters there are, the better your chances to kill them. That same evening, we moved the tent to where the caribou had been seen. Each hunter had his toboggan. We spent the night close to our warm stoves, close to the caribou.

We were up before sunrise. Our guns had been ready since the previous day. We'd also prepared food to eat during the day.

That time, we killed thirty-two caribou. We had a very good supply of meat. In addition, those caribou provided us with a large quantity of grease. Each caribou has eight bones that are used to make grease. Just think how much grease you can get from thirty-two caribou. And you mustn't forget the heads. With the heads of all those caribou, we weren't going to run out of food, that's for sure.

We had only a small amount of flour with us. As I said, it was used only to make broth for the children. When we left Mingan during the summer, we'd have several sacks of flour with us. But we left sacks in various places, on our racks. By that time, in January, we were carrying only a small amount of flour with us. And we guarded that flour preciously. Occasionally, when we returned from a very long walk and a tiring but rewarding hunt, my wife would make a small bannock for the whole family. That was the only time I ate bannock. In my opinion, meat was better. I think all of the hunters agreed with me on that.

Usually, we killed three or four caribou at one time. We preferred the females because we got more grease from them. And you needed this grease if you wanted to make a good meal. A meal without grease is not a real meal!

Yes, that's what it was really like. We weren't always lucky. It was sometimes hard to kill animals, any animal at all. When bad luck struck, one of the hunters was to blame; like, for example, the year we had a hunter from Natashquan in our group. His nickname was Tshishennu, which means "Old Man," but in fact he wasn't all that old.

We were unlucky like never before. I managed to kill a caribou from time to time, but my companion didn't kill any.

I tell you, he was really unlucky. Nonetheless, he was a good hunter and he liked to eat meat.

The next winter I was with François Nolin and Jérôme Napish. Tshishennu was no longer with us, and we had no more problems. That winter, we killed many caribou and never ran out of meat. But François liked to hunt; Jérôme too. They were constantly out tracking caribou, and they regularly brought home porcupines. I did the same. If none was wasted, six porcupines could feed three families for three days.

The problem with Tshishennu was, even though he was a good hunter, he didn't behave like an Indian should behave. He hid his meat from us. If he caught something, he kept it for his family. He didn't care about my family. I also had to feed my family and I nonetheless gave him meat when I had some.

One day he caught a trout and a pike. They were really big fish. Rather than give us a little, like families living on the land always did, he decided to eat the fish in secret with his family. It was Christmas Day.

That morning my family and I didn't have anything to eat. We couldn't see Tshishennu's tent from ours. And I hadn't seen him for two days. We didn't know what he'd been doing. So my godmother went over to visit him. She entered the tent and discovered Tshishennu's wife pounding the liver of a big trout. She asked the woman what she was doing. Tshishennu's wife replied that she was preparing the liver of a fish for her son, Charles. She then added that her husband had been lucky enough to catch a big trout and a big pike. My godmother asked where the fish were. Tshishennu's wife admitted that they had eaten them and that they had none left.

So my godmother said to her, "Don't you know that we're supposed to help each other and share all the food when we're living on the land? The hunters left this morning without eating. We have no more food in our tent. Come and take a look, if you want."

Things continued to go badly, so we decided to head for North West River. Tshishennu was the first to suffer. He was having trouble walking. His mouth had turned black, and his face was frostbitten. He was always cold, even though he was warmly dressed.

On the way to North West River, our luck returned. Every evening I went ahead to break trail for the following day, and each time I killed some porcupines. My grandfather came with me. But rather than walk on the trail, he walked off to the side, keeping up with me all the while. He was thus able to kill some porcupines that I would have missed. It was a good idea. One evening, he joined me on the trail carrying two porcupines on his back. He was tired but he was smiling. Laying down the porcupines, he asked me to wait. He set out in the direction from which he'd just come, and soon reappeared. He was carrying two more porcupines! He had killed four porcupines in no time at all.

Another night, this time when I was out alone, it was my turn to kill four porcupines. They were too heavy for me to carry in one load back to camp. So I buried two in the snow along the trail we were intending to take the next day with our families. I took the other two home with me.

The women weren't catching many rabbits. It was extremely cold and therefore hard to work outside. There weren't many rabbits out of their lairs. The cold was very hard on Tshishennu, who was sick. He could no longer hunt. During the day, when we were traveling, he really suffered. He was too warmly dressed for traveling. He could barely walk. On the days we weren't traveling, Tshishennu stayed in his tent.

We were feeding him—him and his family. Tshishennu almost died. He came very close to not making it all the way to Winuakapau with us. Tshishennu needed bannock, and luckily we found some.

At Winuakapau Lake I met up with an English-speaking trapper. He said to me, "You'll find a lot of flour in Eli Blake's cabin. Eli doesn't need it any more because he went back to North West River, for good. He was sick."

The next day we started walking alongside the Hamilton River in the direction of Eli Blake's cabin. It was a beautiful morning and the snow was hard, which made our work easier. The river is very wide in that area and we were walking close to one shore. The river is so wide you can barely make out the other shore. There was snow as far as you could see.

But we had already spotted Eli Blake's cabin on our side of the river, and that's where we went. He had hidden his flour under his canoe, on a rack. There were several small sacks of flour as well as some buckets full of flour. Then, in his cabin, we found a big chest containing salted meat, lard, tobacco, and sugar.

We set up our tents right beside the cabin. I went into the cabin and lit Eli's big sheet-metal stove. It heated well and would be useful for making bannock.

I knew Eli Blake personally. He'd already told me I could use his cabin if ever my family and I were in trouble. He'd also told me he kept some flour in buckets in case visitors might need it.

So the women made bannock. Tshishennu still hadn't arrived. He walked very slowly and was always falling far behind us. He was very, very sick.

When he arrived at our camp my grandfather warned, "I know that you are very hungry, but you mustn't eat too much. In your condition, you'll make yourself even sicker if you eat too much. You'll become completely paralyzed and get bad diarrhea. And if you become paralyzed we'll have to carry you as well as our packs. We mustn't let that happen."

We were all quite healthy. Tshishennu was the only one who was very sick. It wouldn't have required much food for him to get diarrhea, since he already had it. So we gave him only tiny portions of bannock, and he realized that there'd be enough to last until we got to North West River.

Little by little, day by day, we finally arrived at the ocean. Tshishennu was saved and must have been very glad that he'd made it. But, in the end, he'd brought on his misery. He didn't work enough. When he did get down to it, he was a good hunter. But he didn't like hunting porcupines and would often come back from a hunt with nothing. When he did work a lot, luck smiled on him. But most of the time he didn't hunt enough.

A few days later we left North West River to return to the land. At that point our main interest was hunting caribou. The hunt took us, the men, far away from the family camp for a period of four weeks. While we were away, the women didn't go hungry. They also hunted, as I've already said. They chopped down birch trees. Birches attract rabbits, you know. After cutting the trees, they set snares around them.

A good little hunting dog helped when it came to killing porcupines and grouse. This little dog always walked behind the hunter; otherwise, it tired too quickly from flailing in the snow. A good dog always had its nose to the wind. All you had to do was keep your eye on the dog. If it really wanted to go in a certain direction, it must have caught a scent. So it would leave the hunter's trail and head slowly in that direction, toward the porcupine. Sometimes the dog stopped; it had lost the porcupine's scent because the wind had changed direction for a second or two. The dog waited, without moving, its nose in the air. It was waiting for the wind to turn, to blow directly in its face. As soon as it did, the dog set off again and led us right to the tree in which the porcupine was hiding.

That's a good hunting dog. With a dog like that a hunter had better luck. But the dog had to do its share because some days a good dog didn't feel like hunting. It didn't pick up a scent and instead ran off in all directions, at random.

The women often hunted with dogs. Like we'd advised them, the women didn't walk right up to the porcupine's den, which is the only place where a porcupine becomes dangerous. You couldn't try to force the animal out. It was better to set a trap on the trail leading to its hole.

The men were far away at the time, looking for caribou. We were following a trail, but it was hard going. The caribou were on the move. Several times we came across trails going in every direction and had to decide which way to go. The chase lasted several days. In the evening, we split up the work. Some of us set up the tents and organized a small camp. The others went scouting, to figure out what the caribou were doing. I preferred the scouting, though it meant more walking.

Occasionally, the scouts discovered caribou during their evening walk. They then returned to the camp to tell the others. But we waited until the next day to kill the caribou.

That time we killed forty-six caribou. We were very happy, since it meant we'd have meat for a long time. The caribou were all bled, butchered, and buried under the snow. Burying them was easy because the snow was deep. We then took down our tents so we could go tell our families. When we arrived back at the camp, we told everyone about the kill and announced the coming move. They were all happy to hear the news.

We moved everything to the hunting grounds. We stayed there a month, hunting for furs, now that we'd killed some caribou. We had a lot of meat in reserve and everything was going well. Times were good.

It was essential to have meat. The Elders ate meat. We did, too, we ate nothing but meat and fat. We were used to it. With some flour, salt, sugar, and lard from the store, the hunter tried to get by. We carried as little as possible of these provisions with us. We watched very carefully what we ate, trying to eat very little of these things. The only things a hunter couldn't do without were tea and tobacco. We liked to drink tea and smoke.

When we ran out of these provisions we returned to the coast, to North West River. It wasn't as far away as Mingan. In addition, most of the English-speaking trappers working in the Winuakapau area kept provisions for hunters who'd run out of items other than meat. We could get salt, sugar, lard, flour, tea, and tobacco at their places. We needed these things for ourselves, but especially for our children.

The best thing that could happen was to kill a large number of caribou in one place. Then, we would build racks here and there and go hunt for furs without having to move around too much.

Killing caribou while we were traveling with our families was even better. The women were right there, so the work went twice as fast.

Almost every time we went to North West River, we arrived in January. We'd stay for about fifteen days, sometimes for a month. At the end of the month we'd get ready to start back for Mingan.

By mid-March we'd be about halfway between North West River and Mingan. At that point the families would split up for a while. Two families would go in one direction, the other two somewhere else. The hunters discussed their preferences—where in the area they wanted to go.

This is what sometimes happened to me. We were three families returning from North West River. There was François Nolin, who really loved his tea and tobacco, and Jérôme Napish. As usual in the month of March, we talked about splitting up, and Jérôme and François set off together. I stayed alone with my family. I liked being alone. I was freer and had very good luck while hunting. My supply of caribou meat lasted longer. I always calculated how many days it would take to eat one caribou, and my predictions were always right. But when the others were there, especially Jérôme, they often used up my supply. Jérôme hunted well and worked hard. I enjoyed hunting with him, but he and his family ate a huge amount.

When I was alone I could plan better. Yes, I enjoyed hunting alone with my family on the land. I trapped for furs, since you need several people to hunt for caribou. In March and early April, all of the families went hunting on their own. That lasted one month.

We tried to estimate the price of furs because we wanted to kill enough fur-bearing animals to pay off what we owed the merchant in Mingan.

I think that it took a lot of courage to do what we did. I've known families who were completely demoralized when they arrived back in Mingan because they hadn't found any caribou. When there are no caribou, you have to eat bannock and return to the village for more provisions. But to get your provisions, you have to kill fur-bearing animals. And to do that, you first need to kill caribou. The most important part was the caribou. Without caribou, no one would have had the strength to work as hard as we did.

Caribou meat gives you strength, courage. Caribou are hard to find, but you must find them. Families who don't become demoralized.

When you came across the tracks of a caribou, you had to follow them right to the end, even if the tracks were old. I've followed caribou tracks that were several days old. I was determined to follow them right to the end. If you didn't do that, you became demoralized and your luck ran out. That's why there were families who returned to Mingan during the winter.

Each member of the family had to work very hard. My grandmother Kukuminash hunted porcupines every day. She would go out with one of her granddaughters. She hunted like that until her death. She caught porcupines right up until the day she died. That's the way it was for a woman on the land.

By April, the warm weather was back. That was the time for otters and beavers. The flooding and high water meant that beavers had to take refuge inside their lodges. The water would rise so much that the beaver had to thin out the inside upper walls of the den if it wanted to stay dry. The beaver sometimes thinned them so much that it made holes in the lodge. This made it easy for us to set traps right inside. You could even shoot the beavers with a rifle. If you were lucky, you could kill several beavers in one lodge. That was worthwhile.

At the end of April all the families gathered at the rendez-vous, that is, the place where we'd split up in March. Spring was on its way. The snow was melting.

You couldn't starve in springtime, there were so many animals to kill. But you had to be careful out on the ice and on the rivers. Normally, we were north of Lake Brûlé at that time of year. We were heading down toward Mingan, several families traveling together. We did that so we could help each other in case of accidents. The rivers were dangerous then, and if a canoe capsized in the frigid water you had to help.

If you didn't have as many furs as you wanted, you trapped more while traveling down to Mingan.

You met other families because everyone was returning to Mingan in the month of May, and we always took the same route.

Spring is the best time for catching fish and geese. It's a wonderful time of year. But by spring, we were running short of flour, tea, and tobacco. We helped each other out, knowing that we were almost back at the village.

The merchant in the village, Mister Lawson, sold a particular type of tea—blue tea—and it wasn't any good. It tasted salty. Mister Lawson often asked me if I liked this tea. I told him I'd never had tea that tasted so bad. Even in spring, when we were running short of all our store-bought provisions, I didn't like that blue tea.

My story ends here.

SEVEN

A WORD ON THE **ELDERS**, WORK IN THE **OLD DAYS**, AND **TRADITION**

I'm now going to tell you how the very old Indians, the Elders, went about killing animals.

Otters live in streams. I would plant wooden stakes in a stream to create a barrier for the otter. I wanted to narrow down the otter's path. The otter followed the two rows of stakes, which gradually came closer together and narrowed down the passageway. At the end would be a gap just big enough for the otter, and that's where I set my wooden trap.

Beaver could also be caught with wooden traps. It wasn't too hard. Often, you couldn't catch beaver using a steel trap.

They're an animal that's hard to trap. Time and time again, a beaver would escape with a trap or the trap would snap shut before the beaver stepped on the right spot. The old ways were better for catching animals, but they required a lot of work.

The most effective way to catch a beaver was using a net. I often did that. You had to dam off a section of a lake, at the place where a stream enters the bay, which is where beavers like to build their lodges. As in hunting otter, you had to direct the beaver toward the net. So you staked out a pathway for the animal to follow.

One day I came across a beaver lodge. It was a good place to catch a beaver using a net. That evening, I built a pathway using stakes. And I made a net during the night. You have to make the net at night because beavers work at night. They sleep during the day, dreaming of the net that awaits them. The Elders used to say that, and I really believe it's true.

Once the net was in position, I set out with my dog across the lake. We located all of the beaver's holes and destroyed them. The beaver had only one place to get out of the water, and that was through my net. I had destroyed several openings when someone shouted that the beaver was caught in the net. You see how easy it was.

I learned these methods from the old hunters who had, in turn, learned them from other old hunters. You could also catch otters in a net. The old hunters said that otter and beaver never tried to cut the net with their teeth. And that was true. They were very clever and knew a lot of things, the Elders.

A WORD ON THE ELDERS

But to be successful using their methods, you had to believe in them. You had to be confident. Everyone had certain things that they did out on the land. The only thing that I never did was to catch an otter using a net. Yes, the Elders hunted like that and we followed their ways.

They weren't all magicians, and they didn't spend all of their time in shaking tents. They worked very hard to survive, and they did whatever was necessary to find the food they needed. I did the same, right up until the day I came back to Mingan for good.

A hunter never stopped working. He didn't just walk in a straight line without stopping. He always had his eyes peeled. Caribou and other animals cannot be caught by someone who's a careless hunter. Out on the land, you have to be thinking about caribou all the time.

Let me tell you about something that happened to me. I had purchased a hunting knife in North West River. I planned to use it to butcher caribou. Back at the camp, I had a dream that night. In my dream, my tent was surrounded by caribou tracks. A voice asked me for my knife. This voice changed into a song. Yes, someone was singing in the distance, "It's the caribou who's singing." It was the caribou, no doubt about it.

This dream was part of the hunt. I was thinking about hunting even as I slept.

At dawn I got up. I was out with Sylvestre Nolin. I said to him, "Someone is singing out there, not far away." And we immediately set off. We headed toward a lake I knew well. In my dream, the caribou was singing on that lake.

We didn't have far to go. Well before we saw the lake, I started putting bullets in my rifle. I knew that the caribou would be there. When we got to the lake, we saw several sets of caribou tracks. All over the lake the caribou had pawed the snow, looking for food. Some of the holes were old, others were very fresh.

The caribou was there, right in the middle of the lake. He was fat, he was magnificent. Of course, it was him, the large bull who had sung to me the night before. I fired twice, since he was far away and he was a good runner. And it was the second shot that killed him.

There was an Indian in the vicinity. He heard the gunshots and ran out on the lake. We saw him in the distance. It was my grandfather Damien. He had come from the Naskauekan River. In fact, his camp was located well above the river, at Kanetinat.

When he approached he said, "There are a lot of caribou around Kanetinat, but we still haven't killed a single one. We knew there was a caribou here, and I sent Jérôme to kill it. But he couldn't find it. Now I see that it's you who killed it."

Yes, that's the way it used to be. This caribou had lived alone on the lake since the start of winter. No one had been able to find it. It was my dream that enabled me to kill this caribou; I was supposed to kill him.

The Elders knew how to hunt using their dreams. All of them did. In dreams or in the shaking tent, the caribou spoke to the hunter. The caribou helped a good hunter. But magic isn't everything. A magician can suffer from starvation. His magic can bring him bad luck.

A WORD ON THE ELDERS

To ward off bad luck, the Elders had caribou feasts. I, myself, have often taken part in these feasts.

If caribou had been killed, you set up your camp near the lake where you'd been hunting. The hunters then chose, from among the dead caribou, the nicest and especially the fattest one. It was almost always a female.

Then the feast began. We boiled the hard fat from the caribou with the chest of the animal. What we had boiling in our largest pot was very fatty. The Elders ate a lot of grease; they never worried about eating too much of it. But I never liked to eat a large amount of grease at one time. Still, you had to eat it. The Elders ate every last bit of the grease.

The women took the caribou skin inside the tent and dipped it in water. They then wrung it out and hung it to dry. There could be no more traces of blood on it. They would set up a wooden scraper inside the tent. In the meantime, others would be scraping the meat off the bones of the caribou. There are eight long bones in a caribou. Its head would be hung to roast over the fire. According to tradition, absolutely all of the caribou meat had to be eaten during the feast. Of course, when there were a lot of us, this wasn't hard.

Absolutely everything had to be eaten, even the liver of the caribou. You pounded the liver until it was almost liquid, then added grease and a little sugar, if you had any. Everyone got their share. The feast ended with that. The end of such a feast brought us good luck in the future.

Like us, the Elders hunted fur-bearing animals. They caught a lot of them. They were not forever feasting. They hunted all the animals. I know that the Elders liked to eat huge amounts of grease. During meals, they ate a lot of meat and grease. I preferred eating just a little so that I didn't suffer too much when food was scarce.

In the old days the women worked very fast on the caribou skins. The night after a feast, the women got together to scrape and soften the caribou skin. They worked through the night because they had to finish before dawn. Even before the sun was up, the women came out of the tent with their skin. Each of the four corners of the skin would be painted red. If there was still some caribou grease, it also had to be eaten before dawn.

The skin was left outside for the entire day. We made the red dye with plants we had collected the previous summer. In the evening, when we went to get the skin, the red marks would be bigger. That was the blood of the caribou, and it meant we had a better chance to kill it.

I've seen these things. They are true. You had to do them because, if you didn't, you would never find caribou. The hunter who respected caribou meat had good luck when he hunted. Anyone who wasted it, who carelessly left caribou meat on the snow or whose dogs ate it, that person could expect the worst.

When luck is with a hunter, it doesn't last forever. The hunter must realize that. Surplus meat must always be kept on a rack, well protected by canvas tarps and fir boughs.

The fruit of the hunt is precious. Wasting it is a serious thing. Those who acted as if they'd always be lucky and never run short of meat... they're the ones who starved to death.

A WORD ON THE ELDERS

Waste and lack of foresight always lead to famine. It was always that way out on the land.

In the old days, in the interior and here, around Mingan, there were a lot of caribou. Today, there are almost none. Long ago, when I was living out on the land, I dreamed of what we see happening around us today. I always knew that the caribou would disappear one day. There is not a single caribou living in the vicinity of Magpie Lake, and it used to be known as a place where caribou were plentiful.

We can blame the white hunters for that. They've always hunted like bad Indians. They don't respect the caribou. White hunters kill caribou and then take only the choice pieces with them. They waste the rest, leaving it out on the ice of the lake. If caribou are disappearing, it's because white hunters can't stop this waste. The caribou do to them what they do to us. If we're not careful, the caribou will disappear.

The Elders used to say, "Never waste caribou meat because it's protected by a spirit. The caribou obey their master, Papakassik. If families leave caribou hooves lying around, if the dogs are allowed to eat caribou, the Indians will suffer."

I often heard those very words. There's an old story about this that happened very long ago.

Hunters killed eight caribou. It was during the first snowfall of the winter. They cut off several pieces of meat and returned to camp, leaving the caribou right on the ground where they were. They said that they'd go back later to get them. They planned to wait until the lakes had frozen, to make it easier to move the meat and to shorten their trip. They even broke a trail.

There were four hunters as well as their families. One of them was a magician.

The caribou had been dead for a long time, yet the hunters continued to postpone their return for the meat. One day, two of the four hunters, the oldest ones in the group, started talking about the caribou meat they had left behind. The oldest one said, "I have a feeling that all of this is going to cause us lots of problems." These hunters were real men of the interior lands. One of them was nicknamed Watshekat.

They decided to set up a shaking tent because they wanted to know more about this. They performed the ceremony in the evening. They put up a small tent inside the family tent. Then, the shaman entered the shaking tent and everyone gathered around him. They all heard Papakassik, Master of the Caribou, when he came into the tent. He was in a terrible mood because of the eight wasted caribou. I understand why he was mad; it had been almost a month since the hunters had killed those caribou, and the meat was still back at that place. They should have gone to get it long before, especially since they had already broken a trail to move it.

In the shaking tent the Master of the Caribou made the following speech: "What have you done? I give you food and you don't take it. You leave it lying on the ice or wherever for almost a month."

The Master of the Caribou spoke using the shaman's mouth. Watshekat, the oldest of the hunters, said he became very frightened and urged the others to go get the meat the very next day.

I think they should have gone to get the meat long before, carrying it in packs on their backs like all the Indians who lived out on the land did.

The Spirit of the Caribou, who spoke in the voice of the shaman, continued his speech: "You could at least have brought back the bones of the caribou to make grease for yourselves. You could at least have brought back the caribou skins to make *babiche*. You could also have brought back the heads of the caribou, which are so good to eat. It's important that you make the grease. Everything must be ready for tomorrow, and I insist that all of the grease be eaten the day after that. You will prepare the best of the skins from the female caribou. When everything's ready, I'll give you one day to eat all of the grease from the eight dead caribou. You will eat until there's no more left."

Watshekat was becoming more and more frightened. The grease of the eight caribou would fill a twenty-pound pot!

The Master of the Caribou continued: "You may leave the meat at that place. But you must get it ready and then bury it in the snow. You can go get it later. As for the grease, you must absolutely eat it as soon as possible. If you don't do this, something very serious will happen to all of you."

According to Watshekat, Papakassik's voice was terrifying and everyone was very scared. The hunters immediately started getting ready to bring back the legs of the caribou so they could prepare the grease. They then made a huge amount of grease with the legs of all those caribou. When the broth had cooled, they threw a little snow into the pot and started eating the grease.

No one said anything. The women and the children didn't share in the meal. There was so much grease that the hunters became discouraged. They were frightened. The meal had begun at dawn, and the four hunters had to finish eating it by that evening. The shaman also took part in the meal.

Watshekat tried to think of a solution. It was growing dark when two of the hunters stopped eating. Only half of the grease had been eaten! Watshekat was also a shaman, and he was the oldest of the group. He scraped the grease from the sides of the pot, pushing it onto the large mound in the middle. Concentrating very hard, he told himself that he could eat all of the remaining grease by himself: "If I don't get sick, I'll manage to eat it."

He sprinkled powdered meat on the grease and tasted it. The other three watched him silently. "I think I can manage," Watshekat said, then started eating very fast. The grease disappeared bit by bit as he ate. He didn't stop, and soon there was no more grease in the pot. Now all he had to do was wash the pot. "I must keep down this grease," he said. He swallowed the last bite of grease, cleaned the pot, and told the others to scrub the utensils with moss, then burn the moss. The three other hunters watched Watshekat intently because they were sure he'd get sick.

Watshekat spoke roughly. He threw the pot outside the tent and shouted at one of the hunters, "Here's my pot. See how clean it is now." Watshekat concentrated very hard on not getting sick. He must have had an unusually tough stomach, that man. But he was a shaman, and he probably had some trick to allow him to keep down all that grease. It was an extraordinary feat considering the number of caribou that had been killed and all the grease he had to eat.

Now the worst was over. The families were relieved because they no longer had anything to fear. The very next day they started moving the meat that was still back at that place. It took them two days to finish the job, and then they prepared another shaking tent. The Master of the Caribou also came to it. He wasn't alone. He was accompanied by an interpreter, the spirit known as Tshimushumapeu. Tshimushumapeu told the shaman what the Master of the Caribou was saying.

But it was the shaman who began by speaking to the Master of the Caribou, "We have eaten all of the grease. What will happen to us now? Will we have good luck?"

The spirit said to him, "Nothing will happen to you. I'm very pleased with your behavior. You ate the grease and brought back the meat. And you cleaned the pot especially well. From now on I'll help you in the hunt and I'll provide you with caribou. But never again do what you did."

I wonder why Watshekat, who was old and was a magician, didn't warn the other hunters of the dangers of provoking the Master of the Caribou. Watshekat certainly knew all of those things. He must have known that wasting caribou meat is the worst thing a hunter can do.

After these events, the four families went back to their normal lives. They moved on, to hunt for porcupines and go fishing. Soon after the ice forms on the lakes is when hunters can do a lot of fishing.

According to the Elders, there are very few bears in the forest. We were not supposed to kill a lot of bears. The old hunters said we must never kill too many bears.

One day I was out with Mathias. We had killed a bear the week before, and there in front of us was the den of another bear. Mathias said to me, "Let's leave it be. We won't kill it." We had enough meat from the bear we'd killed several days earlier.

Bears were the only animals that our Elders told us not to kill too many of. They were probably right. Because Bear is to some extent a friend, he's very close to man. Bear lived with an Indian in his den for a winter or two. This man couldn't walk.

The Elders told us these stories. We heard a lot about the Indian who lived with his grandfather, the Bear. The Elders knew a lot of things before they became Catholics. They were strong and clever.

They invented and built a very unusual kind of beaver trap. When they located a beaver lodge, they destroyed all of the holes and blocked all of the openings to the lodge. They then made a hole in the lodge about the size of a beaver and placed a trap in this gap. The trap was in fact a kind of enclosure. When the beavers left the lodge—there were sometimes five or six of them—the hunter closed the trap and the beavers were caught. The floor of the enclosure would be covered with moss in the summer. The beavers didn't suspect a thing. One hunter made sure the trap was firmly attached to the lodge, the other was in charge of closing the trap. This type of hunting was done at night.

A WORD ON THE ELDERS

The Elders were very crafty. We hunted like them because we had learned, from one generation to another, their old methods. As a boy I learned mostly by hunting alongside two Elders. They were already very old when I was just little. They knew a lot of things. The first of them was my grandfather Joseph. His nickname was Little Joseph. He was very old but he still hunted. In winter, he captured live beavers by reaching down into freezing water and grabbing them. He picked them up by the tail or the feet. I did that all my life and I taught my sons this, too. To catch a beaver this way, you have to know how to read its movement in the water while looking through a hole in the ice. The water breathes at the rhythm of the beaver. If the water isn't moving, it means there's no beaver nearby. A good hunter knows, by the movement of the water in his hole, where the beaver is under the ice on the lake. And he knows when that beaver will pass by his hole. That's when he can grab it with his hands and pull it out. Some hunters were very good at this.

You see what good hunters they were. They had all sorts of other ways to kill animals. The Elders didn't like it if you made the beaver bleed from the nose. They often used traps made from wooden poles that broke a beaver's back. You could hear the sound of the trap snapping closed from far away. These traps were very effective, day and night. I knew how to hunt using the old methods, and I often hunted that way.

One day I was hunting with my grandfather Sylvestre. We were out alone, hunting beaver. Thaddée and the others were back at the camp, which wasn't far away. My wife was also there. I'm talking about my first wife, the mother of my daughter Marie, who is today married to Edmond Napish.

It was late autumn. The lake was small and we were working above it on one side, on one of the beaver dams. We had built a wooden trap. I'd also set a steel trap. A beaver had sprung it and managed to escape, dragging it with him. He had headed down the hill toward the lake. You know, steel traps aren't nearly as good as people say they are. I climbed down the hill and waited for the beaver. I could hear it coming—hear the sound of the trap banging against rocks and trees. I shot the beaver with my rifle.

As I was climbing back up to the dam where we were working, my dog came across three two-year-old beavers trying to escape. The wooden trap on the beaver dam had failed because the pieces of wood had frozen. The trap released too early. My grandfather said to me, "We'll spend the night here and leave when those three beavers have been killed. Take the trap apart and thaw it out over a fire."

Firewood was hard to find; nonetheless, we succeeded in getting the trap to work the way it was supposed to. And in the morning we killed all of the beavers. Wooden traps were a lot more effective than steel ones, which would freeze up even worse than the wooden type. I often killed beaver with wooden traps.

My grandfather was extremely good at it. He almost never used steel traps during his lifetime. I don't think he even owned any. You have to remember that steel traps are very heavy to carry long distances.

Yes, I knew the Elders, and they taught me a lot of things. In my day all of the hunters learned their skills from them. My grandfather Little Joseph, the one who was so skilled, often told me about his uncle. He said that his uncle was the best hunter he'd ever known. His nickname was Mistakau. I had another grandfather who also taught me the old methods. His name was Kashupe. He was also very knowledgeable. That's the way they were, the Elders.

They could hunt otter by tapping the ice and keeping an eye on the air holes. The Indians who were the very best at hunting otter this way were the Indians from the tundra. Pashin told me that because he'd spent one winter hunting with them. Pashin often told my grandfather the story and I listened as he talked. When he was out hunting with the Indians of the tundra, he wondered how they caught otters using such an unusual method.

Pashin listened to what the Indians from the tundra said, and he also watched them. That's how he learned. The Indians made noise on the ice of a big lake. They tapped the surface with poles and the otter tried to escape by swimming away. But they were actually leading the otter on. They had made holes in the ice farther along, and they tried to head the otter in that direction. When the animal got there, it had no choice but to come to the surface to breathe at the holes, where hunters were waiting for it.

Pashin said the method worked very well on a big lake, but on a small one, the otter always managed to get away. It would hide in a hole, then escape into the woods without the hunters seeing it. On a big lake, the Indians of the tundra could always figure out toward which shore the otter was headed. But the otter couldn't swim all the way without coming up to the surface to breathe, and then it was easy to kill it.

Pashin and my grandfather used this method, and they did very well. How had the Indians of the tundra come up with such a method? They never hunted otter using nets. Neither did I. But I saw my grandfather do it.

He first blocked a stream by laying a wooden pole across it from one side to the other. Attached to this pole was the net, which was stretched across the width of the stream, underwater. The otter swam down the stream. It came to the pole and, instead of going over it, dove underwater to pass under it. It would then get caught in the net. Otters always did that.

My grandfather told me he usually caught pairs of otters with nets.

Beavers are strong. They can get out of a net if they fight hard enough. But otters will never get away. This was the way the Elders hunted.

Most of the time they used wooden traps. The traps for otters and for beavers were exactly the same, except that the inside of the beaver trap was four inches larger. And with the beaver trap, the wooden pole that was supposed to fall on the animal's back was set higher. Beavers have round backs and they are slow. Otters are fast and, to catch them, the wooden pole has to fall very quickly. Otherwise, the otter will be gone before the pole falls, even if the trap works as it should.

Killing animals this way was pretty exciting. We were very proud as we watched our wooden traps catch beavers. My greatest accomplishment in using this method was to trap two otters at the same time with a single trap. They were running side by side. The first one was hit across its back by the pole, the second one, on the head.

That's how the Elders used to hunt. We followed in their footsteps because their methods were good. I often hunted the same way the Elders did and it worked very well. The other hunters did the same.

My grandfather taught me to catch bears using a trap at Manitou Lake, near here. I found the trigger mechanism very complicated. So we built a bear trap together. We put bait on the trigger—beaver kidneys. The bear came along and walked into the trap. When it reached out to the kidneys with its front paw, it released the trigger. But our trap wasn't well made. Instead of hitting the bear on the head, the pole came down on its back paw. My grandfather said, "I set the wooden pole too high." In addition, the bear was standing upright in the trap. The pole couldn't have hit it on its back. In fact, the pole fell on the bear's back but, because the bear was upright, rolled onto its foot. All the same, it was caught. But the bear was far from dead. It looked straight ahead, and we could see that its leg was hurting. It wanted to get out. It must have been saying to itself, "I can escape if I can free my leg." But the trap held firm. The bear fought desperately. It broke everything within reach. It dug holes in the ground. It uprooted small trees.

My grandfather had put two big rocks there to prevent the poles from rolling away. If he hadn't done that, the bear would no doubt have worked itself free. It chewed on the wooden posts. In the end, it was so exhausted that it died. It was a very big bear. If the pole had hit it across the back, the bear wouldn't have suffered. Those deadfalls, those poles, were very heavy. When the trap was well made, it was very effective. The Elders were good workers.

The lives of the Elders were very different from the lives of the whites. Look how the whites live today.

When I was young, we heated our tents with fire rocks. We didn't yet have those little sheet-metal stoves, though the whites already had double box stoves in their houses.

In the old days, here in Mingan, which is on the coast, there were many traces of those fires. You could see the rocks that had been used when we camped here. I don't know if you've ever seen one. They are all over on the land, especially in places that were easily accessible by canoe and where we often camped back then. Yes, in the old campsites, you always see traces of fire rocks.

Making a good fire rock in winter was hard, but it was important. If you wanted a rock to heat really well, you first had to let it cool off. Then you picked up the little hunting dog that stayed inside the tent with us and scratched lines on the rock with the nails on one of its paws. Then you rekindled the fire to reheat the rock. When it had grown very hot again, the rock cracked along the lines traced on it with the dog's nails. You then picked up sticks and hit the lines on the rock. The Elders showed us that. This made the rock heat better than ever. It worked really well.

I lived in a tent like that with my grandfather. It was the fire rock that kept us warm. We were very comfortable and never got cold. With those little stoves, the old people always got cold. But in the old days, with our fire rocks, it was warm in our tents, even when it was extremely cold.

The coals and smoldering logs made strange shadows on the inside of the tent. It was very beautiful. It was our light.